BE
EXTRAORDINARY!

Crush Mediocrity   Spark Curiosity

T0204451

JUSTIN
HONAMAN

All comments and direct quotes are the writer's interpretation of speeches, presentations, discussions, and/or written material.

BE EXTRAORDINARY!

CRUSH MEDIOCRITY. SPARK CURIOSITY.

Published by Justin Honaman

Copyright 2012 by Justin Honaman

International Standard Book Number: 978-0-9882547-1-8

Cover design and editing by Henderson Shapiro Peck

Printed in the United States of America

For more information, visit: WWW.HONAMAN.COM

MY MISSION

To make a positive difference.

CONTENTS

"To laugh often and much;

to win the respect of intelligent people and the affection of children;

to earn the appreciation of honest critics and endure
the betrayal of false friends;

to appreciate beauty, to find the best in others;

to leave the world a bit better, whether by a healthy child,
a garden patch or a redeemed social condition;

to know even one life has breathed easier because you lived.

This is to have succeeded."

— Ralph Waldo Emerson

INTRODUCTION

"Extraordinary leadership is the ability to see beyond yourself; to see the future; and to cast a clear and compelling vision for how to get there."

– Matt Stevens, VP, Professional Services, CBeyond

And so it begins ... again!

If you are not prepared to make big change, to pursue big change, to encourage big change, or to lead *extraordinary* change, then this book is not for you.

If you are not prepared to try new leadership techniques, to engage your team, to challenge the organization, to think global and act local, to communicate in new and different ways, to challenge the system thinking, or to develop invested, personal relationships with others, then this book is not for you.

If you are fearful of making tough decisions, cutting against the company culture or attempting to raise the bar beyond artificial thresholds set by an organization that is rarely moving forward, then this book is not for you.

If you are *comfortable* and not interested in progressing,

in taking on the next challenge, in achieving more for the betterment of others, then this book is not for you.

If you are not *curious* and lack the will to pursue your *creative curiosity*, then don't waste your time. And most importantly, if you are turned-off by enthusiasm and positive thinking, close this book and move on. This book is not for you.

This book is centered on one key concept: *Extraordinary Leadership*. This involves making a positive difference. Crafting the future. Pouring positive energy into others with whom you work, play, and interact regularly. Adding significance to your life and the lives of others. Leading, not managing. Going above and beyond. Turning difficult situations and circumstances into positive ones. Forming partnerships that win. Delivering results that surpass expectations. Connecting others in a way that is beneficial and, at times, immeasurable. Empowering a team to achieve successes never before imagined. Coaching individuals to make wise choices and to seek the exceptional. Extending trust and receiving trust in return. Putting people above profits, and recognizing that investing in people drives profits. Rejecting mediocrity as an acceptable form of living, working, acting, or behaving. Crushing mediocrity and sparking creativity in the pursuit of the extraordinary.

The following pages hold insights and advice on how to be extraordinary while making a positive difference as an individual. This could be within the context of your role as a leader, your role in your organization, and/or even your role within a collaborative partnership.

We begin with you. This is all about your personal brand and the elements of people leadership that make you someone others desire to have as their leader. This is what defines you and how you leverage these qualities to make a positive difference. We transition to your organization. This is all about the extraordinary team and the actions you can take as the leader to move the organization beyond ordinary and towards extraordinary. Lastly, we highlight your relationships. This is all about how you craft extraordinary partnerships within and outside of the four walls of your organization; namely with your peers, colleagues, business partners, consultants, contractors, and industry colleagues.

Each chapter starts with a **Big Idea**, expands into a **Core Message**, transitions into **Life Application**, and concludes with a **Bottom Line**. This framework is consistent in each chapter within the book. You will also find quotes from my network of friends and colleagues mixed into each chapter. I asked each to answer this statement: *"Extraordinary leadership is . . . ."* The perspectives are interesting, not only in their content, but also in the diversity of thought offered on the definition of *extraordinary* leadership.

Let's make it happen. It's time to be extraordinary. Time to crush mediocrity. Time to spark curiosity.

EXCEPTIONAL. REMARKABLE.
PHENOMENAL. UNUSUAL.
IMPACTFUL. INCOMPARABLE.
WONDERFUL. NOTABLE. MARVELOUS.
LIMITLESS. FANTASTIC. CURIOUS.
OUTSTANDING. DIFFERENTIATED.
OVER-THE-TOP. UNCOMMON.
SINGULAR. SURPRISING. SPECIAL.
ASTONISHING. RARE. UNIQUE.
UNPRECEDENTED. AMAZING. VIVID.
STRONG. MEMORABLE. INCREDIBLE.
AN ANOMALY.

**A DECISION. A CHOICE.
THAT'S EXTRAORDINARY.**

CHAPTER 1

BIG IDEA!
YOU ARE YOUR OWN BRAND

"Extraordinary leadership is getting others to believe in something bigger than themselves. The leader, however, must first set the example. If he believes in something bigger than himself, others will follow."

– Tony Barnhart, College Football Host, Writer, and Analyst, CBS Sports

---

People tell me that I am that guy who operates best with many proverbial balls in the air – none of which may be dropped and all of which are made of glass. I am full of energy. I enjoy juggling competing priorities – work, personal, community, spiritual and philanthropic commitments. I am always on the go and never miss a beat. I am driven. I am focused on people and results. I am passionate. And I don't like to be told that something is unachievable. I like to make things happen. This is my brand.

I am passionate about making a difference, giving back, and helping others. I like being in the middle of the action with the opportunity to create a vision – and then turn it into a reality. I am passionate about using my talents and skills to better my community and our world. I like to positively influence others. I thrive on the happiness of others and love bringing a smile to the face of a stranger. I am passionate about the personal and professional development of those that I have the opportunity to lead. I feed off the positive energy of others. I am a connector, a mixer, and I value relationships.

I hover between structure and white space. I'm an engineer and I'm creative. I like the structure of project plans and process methodology. I enjoy the creativity of writing song lyrics, melodies, books, and blogs. I am both left-brained and right-brained.

I put my heart into relationships and people, and I wear my emotions on my sleeve. I believe in leading through others. I believe in putting people over profits. And that when I engage and encourage people, the bottom line will inherently grow. I avoid negative energy and the individuals that breed negative thoughts and ideas. I challenge the way that *things have always been done* and strive for something beyond mediocre.

In 2008 I released my first book, *Make It Happen! Live Out Your Personal Brand*, in which I outlined a high-level model for thinking of yourself as a brand. The concept of personal branding has become more and more important as the economy erratically changes and continues to fluctuate. Companies place more value on skilled players and top performers as talent management leaders become more prescriptive with their wants and needs in filling strategic organizational roles.

Your personal brand consists of many things: knowledge, experiences, personality, friends, family, accomplishments, failures, attire, verbal and non-verbal communication, attitude, values, faith, and much more. The equity or value of your personal brand increases or decreases over time, based on *actions taken* and *decisions made* in both personal and professional situations. Think of your personal brand as a bank account: you make *deposits* when you invest in yourself and others, and you make *withdrawals* when you make poor decisions, take actions that intentionally hurt others, or fail to serve as a role model in your position as a leader.

Personal branding is who you are, what's inside, and how that translates to everyday actions, behaviors, and decisions. Studies show that more than 50% of *others'* perception of you upon first meeting you is based on visual image. After visual image, 40% is based on your presentation, posture, and non-verbal actions. 10% or less is based on your actual words. We are going to cover a number of topics in the area of personal branding. The bottom line is that you are your own brand and the value of your brand equity directly translates to the value of the team, organization, company, culture, and environment in which you work and live.

BRINGING IT TO LIFE

◉ **Other's Perception Of Me:** Ask yourself these questions: *What words would my business colleagues use to describe me? What words would my family and friends* *use to describe me?* In fact, instead of you answering for yourself, how about asking others to answer these *about you?* Try it. Know the book on you … and the story you want to tell.

◉ **Brand Investment:** Think of what steps you take to regularly invest in yourself as you answer these questions. *What do I do that increases the value of my personal brand over time? What do I do that decreases the value of my personal brand over time?* Leaders are continually investing in their brand by engaging in training, learning, developing, coaching, and mentoring others.

◉ **My "Work" Brand:** As you think about your current professional role, answer these questions: *How is my current position, role, or project challenging me? Which activities or initiatives am I participating in that are growing my career?* Extraordinary leaders are not satisfied with the status quo and always desire to make a positive difference.

◉ **Speaking Opportunities:** As you prepare to present to a group, you are naturally forced to validate your knowledge of facts and figures, big ideas, and bottom lines. You are also forced to consider not only what is interesting about your content, but also what *others* will find interesting about your content. More importantly, your ability to communicate effectively helps elevate your personal brand. The only way to strengthen this aspect of your brand is through practice. *Are you taking advantage of every possible opportunity to speak in front of others? Does your public speaking "brand" convey knowledge and confidence?*

◉ **Personal Advisory Board:** Create and maintain a list of individuals that you refer to as your *personal advisory board.* These are individuals that provide extraordinary insight, advice, and recommendations, and who span your personal, business, community, and philanthropic interests. You do not need to hold formal *board* meetings but instead, engage each individual with regular check-ins. They know the *book on you* and will always provide transparent and constructive feedback, coaching, and advice. They serve as a grounded reference point. *Who would you say serves on your personal board of advisors?*

BOTTOM LINE
Personal brand value translates into organizational value.

EXCEPTIONAL. REMARKABLE.
PHENOMENAL. UNUSUAL.
IMPACTFUL. INCOMPARABLE.
WONDERFUL. NOTABLE. MARVELOUS.
LIMITLESS. FANTASTIC. CURIOUS.
OUTSTANDING. DIFFERENTIATED.
OVER-THE-TOP. UNCOMMON.
SINGULAR. SURPRISING. SPECIAL.
ASTONISHING. RARE. UNIQUE.
UNPRECEDENTED. AMAZING. VIVID.
STRONG. MEMORABLE. INCREDIBLE.
AN ANOMALY.

**A DECISION. A CHOICE.
THAT'S EXTRAORDINARY.**

CHAPTER 2

BIG IDEA!
MAKING YOUR MARK

"Extraordinary leadership is exactly that: leading.
Being strong enough and having enough faith to not follow
the herd and not leaving well enough alone."

– "Mama" Jan Smith, Owner, Jan Smith Studios, Inc.;
Homegirl Music Publishing; 46Ten, Inc.

Extraordinary leaders consistently ask themselves: *Am I making a difference? Am I making a positive impact? Am I leading change? Am I contributing to the growth of an organization? Am I regularly coaching or mentoring others and helping them to grow in their careers? Am I making my mark?*

At times, your mark is an obvious one. It is recognized and celebrated because it is viewed as an imprint on society, an organization, or an individual. At other times, your mark may not be as obvious, apparent, or readily visible – for example, when you invest time with children, when you coach, mentor or provide advice to others, or even when you spend quality time with a friend or stranger. The mark you make may not be evident until long after you are gone.

The reality is that in relationships, you never really know the mark you leave.

The first step in making your mark is believing in yourself. You must know the settings on your moral compass. You must take a stand and have an opinion based on facts. As I shared in *Make It Happen!* I was criticized several times during my early days in management consulting for always trying to make everyone happy. One of my colleagues referred to this as being *Switzerland*. This phrase evokes an interesting analogy because Switzerland wants to be everyone's friend and is neutral on most international political situations.

People never knew where I stood on a topic or decision because I was always trying to say the *right* thing. I learned very quickly that I drew more respect, appreciation, and followers by taking a stand. I shared my thoughts, ideas, and opinions in a way that was directional, but also did not run over people or intentionally hurt others. This requires *tact* which I define as making a point, observation, or conclusion without intentionally hurting others.

During a major company acquisition and integration with which I was involved, our new CEO stepped on stage to share his thoughts and cast his vision for the business. He closed by answering questions that team members from the newly formed organization had submitted on 3x5 cards. As he read one card, he stopped, paused, and said "This one bothers me. The question is,

'Will we still have half-day Fridays in the summer?'" This had been a former policy in one of the business areas. His response was classic and forever will be etched in my memory. Without missing a beat, he said, "As an organization, we have men and women who work 24/7. They literally carry the weight of our business on their shoulders. If they are working, we are working. We are one company now." The decision was clear. It was not emotional. It struck me as a great example of making a point with tact, given the sensitivity inherent in a post-integration *people* environment.

The reality is that it is not possible to please everyone. And when you try, you will only succeed in *not* making tough decisions and *avoiding* confrontations with situations and people that should be addressed immediately and directly.

BRINGING IT TO LIFE

◉ **The Pleaser:** *Are you one that always strives to make others happy? Someone that avoids conflict or procrastinates on providing timely, direct, constructive feedback?* While it is good to consider the feelings of others, it is also important not to lose an opportunity to help an individual, team, or organization move forward. Mediocrity will fester unless addressed quickly and directly.

◉ **The Communicator:** *What investments are you making to validate your communication style? Do you present regularly to groups, teams, or organizations?*

How often do you request feedback on your presentation or communication skills? Are you a trusted advisor to others? Extraordinary leaders master all forms of communication: written, verbal, and non-verbal. They also serve as a trusted advisor to others and know that loose lips sink *relation-ships.*

◉ **The Tactical Brand Owner:** *When you define "wins" at work, do you only think in terms of individual performance objectives?* A *win* could certainly be defined as a business objective, but a personal *win* might also be taking the first step toward joining Toastmasters. It might be raising your hand and offering to lead the next Six Sigma project. It could be offering to pull together the agenda for the next leadership team meeting. And it might be finally making the decision to pull aside a colleague to offer coaching that you have withheld in the past. From a personal perspective, a small *win* might be ensuring you are home for dinner three nights a week. It could be avoiding the out-of-town weekend trip so that you can be at your son's baseball game. It could be surprising your spouse on his/her birthday. Or it could be simply *asking* more and *assuming* less.

BOTTOM LINE
Your mark is your legacy!

CHAPTER 3

BIG IDEA!
PIONEERING

"When I think of true leadership, it is all about the impression you make on people. It is about the impact you have on them while 'in the moment' and, just as important, what you leave behind for them to remember. In our organization, it is called the WOW factor and, quite simply, it is the comment that is made when you leave a stage, office, sales call, or any other venue where you have made an impression on a person or persons. The question we always ask is 'What did they say as soon as you left the room. Was it WOW or Whatever?'"

— Bob Somers, Vice President, Global Sales, Delta Air Lines

I opened the top cabinet of my desk recently to search for an old notebook. As I did so, a Davy Crockett coonskin cap fell out. Why in the world would I have a coonskin cap in my office, you ask? Great question!

In 2003 I joined a newly created organization. At one of our very first team meetings, the leader gave each of us a Davy Crockett-style coonskin cap and stated, "We are pioneers!" I thought this was interesting … well, sort of. But it was different, and hey, it was my first coonskin cap!

At the time, I had a small idea of what his *pioneer* reference meant, as our group was a newly created organization. New teams were being formed, employees were being migrated from a larger corporate entity, and different routines were being established. If you read the formal definition of *pioneer*, it includes starting something new, treading new paths, and pursuing new, undiscovered territories. It wasn't until 3-4 years later that I fully understood the pioneering concept laid out by that leader. He framed up a vision that included all of us serving as pioneers in creating, establishing, and building this new organization.

Our group was originally chartered with funding for three years. Our business priorities were centered on a limited set of national projects that, once completed, were to signal the end of our organization and a transition into new roles within the business. That didn't happen. Today, the organization is growing. It continues to receive project requests and has engaged in strategic initiatives that were not even considered in scope when originally conceived. The organization continues to grow and adds strategic value many years after its founding.

Even more interesting is that the original culture was one typical of a new organization being formed with bits and pieces of other organizations. It was comprised of new hires and leadership with varied backgrounds, interests, and beliefs. Today the culture is unique, and centers on core tenets such as trust, engagement, investment in employees, communication, passion, delivery excellence, and, of course, fun! In looking back, not every plan worked out. But those closed doors eventually lead to positive organizational change and enabled resources to begin work on other new initiatives.

Pioneers are also bold. They require thick skin – solid armor to protect them against the jealous arrows and lazy left hooks from arrogant, silver-tongued, and self-proclaimed organizational leaders. Boldness quickly fleshes out insecurity, lack of self-confidence, and laziness in others within an organization. After all, if one person is going to be bold and raise the bar, others must follow or risk being left behind, or left out altogether. There is a way to be bold without being brash. Boldness is a trait that is often *suppressed* and often *criticized*. And yet it is a trait that, if cultivated properly, yields extraordinary leadership results.

Being organizational pioneers is not easy and requires significant commitment to a vision that is often not clear to others. It requires the establishment of routines, setting and prioritizing expectations, delivering results, and often making bold decisions quickly to move the organization along the path of development and growth. It also requires finding the *right* people to cut a new path through uncharted territory.

BRINGING IT TO LIFE

◉ **Pioneers Expect To Take Risks**: A number of my friends are true entrepreneurs who have started their own businesses. This required incredible flexibility, creativity, and risk. Most of them are heading toward a successful future. All worked for large corporations before deciding to make the jump to do their own thing. Becoming a pioneer is never easy. It does not come without compromise. Pioneers first weigh the risks and rewards, and then take advantage of the extraordinary opportunities.

How would you rate your tolerance for risk?

◉ **Pioneers Seek The Undiscovered**: What is certainly true of any start-up or new organization is that the future is truly undiscovered territory. Your path will be different by default. While others may have tread a similar path with many lessons learned, the people, processes, technology, and outside influences will be completely different for you. The *fuel* that drives momentum is the *passion* that seeks the undiscovered. Recognizing that there will be boulders (roadblocks), sinkholes (surprises/ changes) and plenty of bad weather (naysayers, non-supporters, doubters, detractors) along the trek will help you prepare to survive the journey. *Does this sound like an environment meant for you?*

◉ **Pioneers Are Impatient With Status Quo:** Pioneers are impatient with mediocrity. They avoid those that seek the obligatory 9 to 5 job; those who operate with an entitlement mentality, and, instead, seek to surround themselves with individuals willing to put in the extra effort to achieve extraordinary – who believe in and are excited about the vision. Pioneers explore uncharted territories and love finding solutions to problems unsolved by others. Pioneers seek out and conquer big challenges.

BOTTOM LINE

Pioneers live life without remorse for lost opportunity.

CHAPTER 4

BIG IDEA!
EMBRACE CHANGE.
CHALLENGE THE PROCESS.

"True leadership is God-given vision, commitment, faith,
and sacrifice. It is knowing when to follow and saying, 'I'm in this until
I am successful, and I will pay any price to make it happen.'"

– Elisabeth Omilami, CEO, Hosea Feed the Hungry
and Homeless; Actress; Human Rights Activist

Challenge the process. Challenge the system thinking. Challenge the norm.

Change is rarely easy. It's frequently rejected and feared. Not surprisingly, as any large organization or process grows, it tends to revert to less risky actions and behaviors. The organization is also less willing to accept new ideas; especially those that fall outside of a typical process framework. Similarly, as leaders develop in their careers, they often revert to safe mode versus challenge mode in fear of risking their future on career-limiting moves. People are naturally averse to change, in fear of breaking something that is working, upsetting the political apple cart, or hurting those that developed the process initially. The natural reaction to change is resistance.

Challenge always precedes any sort of extraordinary change and the status quo will always push back on your big "change" ideas. But in order to initiate extraordinary change, the process must be challenged. Leaders must bring creativity and innovation into play when outlining *new* methods of doing things differently, thus providing *new fuel* to a brand, product, process, or strategic idea.

Consider the following scenario. We were pursuing a business opportunity with a major retailer. It was an opportunity that could clearly generate several million dollars in incremental revenue and gross profit for the retailer's business. However, the retailer declined numerous invitations to meet with us. Instead, they provided many excuses and were slow to respond to calls and emails. They refused to coordinate calendars or even review the opportunity. We were then told, "Our business is going so well that nobody wants to try anything new, or be open to change. Nobody wants to disturb anything because we are growing, opening stores, and generating great financial results. Nobody wants to be the one that did something wrong." Shocking … but not surprising. If you are not open to new growth opportunities, you will never realize any incremental financial or qualitative wins that come from trying something new.

Another example can often be found in the management of successful brands. As a brand manager, there is a pervasive fear of doing anything to mess it up, as opposed to trying new strategies for differentiating and growing the brand. The brand manager often instills his or her own *fear* roadblocks into the situation that often prevent experimentation and trial of new strategies that could lead to significant growth.

As the leader of a team, organization, or group, it is your responsibility to set the pace and establish the change tolerance *guardrails* within which the team should operate. When you recognize and celebrate actions that have driven change, those actions and behaviors will not only be repeated, but will also be followed by others who were more hesitant to be bold.

BRINGING IT TO LIFE

- **Be Out In Front:** As the leader driving change, be ahead of the change process. Recognize that change begins with something new, a triggering event, or a strategic decision. The team and/or organization will typically walk through the denial, fear, anxiety, and misdirected energy phases before hitting a solid state of transition. The final phases of any major change are acceptance, trust, and execution. Typically, every team experiences these phases. What's different is the amount of time spent in each phase, and how leadership influences that time. *Are you helping your team navigate through change quickly? Or are you stifling change out of fear?*

- **Be Clear On Why:** If you are going to drive big change, you must be very clear as to why it makes

sense in your vision. It may not be as obvious
to others. The business case for change may go
beyond numbers and bottom lines, and may truly
be a qualitative benefit. If you are leading change,
you must be grounded in your vision as to why it
makes sense. You will be the one casting the vision.
Know why it is a priority and why you are going to
lead it. *Are you able to clearly articulate the reason for
the change? If not, why should anyone feel compelled to
follow you?*

◉ **Expect Roadblocks:** The organization or team will
naturally acquiesce and push for things to remain
the same. They may formally and informally place
roadblocks in the way of progress. These could be
in the form of delays in responding or appealing to
senior executives as to why the status quo is a better
option. *What's your plan for anticipating and dealing
with roadblocks?* A good change plan is always
enabled by a good strategic communication plan.
How is your communication plan structured?

◉ **Take It Off-Road:** Inevitably, if you are a
high-octane performer, you are going to take it
off-road. Explore new paths to achieve the vision.
Do things differently. Introduce big change or
new thinking. Provide coaching and a level of
transparent communication that are outside of
company standards. The trick is to challenge the
system without bursting through organizational

guardrails. *Are you taking it off-road or are you settling for the status quo?*

◎ **When You Take It Off-Road, Take The High Road:** When you do take it off-road, be sure to take the high road by making the right decisions for your internal customers and your business. That way you will ensure that you maintain the level of trust developed with your customers and colleagues. *Are you acting with the best interests of your people and your organization in mind?*

BOTTOM LINE

Don't settle for the status quo.
Change is your ally.

EXCEPTIONAL. REMARKABLE.
PHENOMENAL. UNUSUAL.
IMPACTFUL. INCOMPARABLE.
WONDERFUL. NOTABLE. MARVELOUS.
LIMITLESS. FANTASTIC. CURIOUS.
OUTSTANDING. DIFFERENTIATED.
OVER-THE-TOP. UNCOMMON.
SINGULAR. SURPRISING. SPECIAL.
ASTONISHING. RARE. UNIQUE.
UNPRECEDENTED. AMAZING. VIVID.
STRONG. MEMORABLE. INCREDIBLE.
AN ANOMALY.

**A DECISION. A CHOICE.
THAT'S EXTRAORDINARY.**

CHAPTER 5

BIG IDEA!
SENSE OF URGENCY

"Extraordinary leadership is measured by a leader's capacity
to set a persistent example of moral integrity and limitless
accountability to his or her team."

– Greg Foster, CEO, BrightWhistle

---

*Why am I the only one who feels this is a priority?! Why
am I the only one who is working to get the proposal out
today and not tomorrow? Why am I the only one who is
pushing to have the contract draft done today and not a week
from today?* Have you ever felt alone in the pursuit of
getting things done quickly? You are working overtime
to get a project out the door while a key member of
your team leaves at 4:59 pm with an *I'm sure it can wait
until tomorrow* attitude. A day lost is a day lost. And a
day lost could be a day of significant *cost increase* or
revenue loss.

Recently, one of my customers told me that a
competitive partnership differentiator, above many
others, was the ability to respond *quickly*. He insisted
on fast follow-up and follow-through. He wanted us to

respond completely and consistently. There is nothing worse than a lack of responsiveness or waiting for internal process delays to negatively affect the effort of getting a partnership off the ground.

How do you move the process quickly? How do you avoid the political hurdles and pitfalls of getting things done that beset any organization, big or small? How do you move consecutive processes into parallel processes to cut down on the time required to get a proposal, contract, or solution back to a customer? And how do you collaborate with your internal support teams to drive fast action? How do you achieve an environment that is solutions-oriented versus one that is centered only on problems and the reasons things cannot get done? How do you effectively convey priorities as "urgent" and differentiate them from others that have additional runway? Would your customers describe your turnaround time as extraordinary? Would you describe your process as well-oiled and efficient?

Regardless of your answers to those questions, any and all processes have room for improvement. The first people to feel the pressure are the front-line employees managing a customer relationship. They feel the daily *burn* or *angst* in their desire to make things happen quickly for the customer.

The key to success is instilling an organizational framework that engages and incents *all* members of the team to over-deliver (and at a minimum meet defined commitments). Whether or not a team member deals with the day-to-day customer interactions, they still must operate with the same sense of urgency as customer-facing individuals.

BRINGING IT TO LIFE

◉ **Be Impatient With The Process:** If your goal is to win new business, every day is another day without a signed contract. Meanwhile, the competition could be in the customer's office pitching their program. Every day is a lost sale for *this* year. Every day is a day of lost revenue and gross profit to your partner who sells your product, and to you as the supplier of the product. If you manage strategic projects, every day is a day *closer* to rollout. Closer to going live. Closer to sunsetting a costly old piece of technology. Every day is one less day in the project plan to work through and resolve tasks, requests, requirements, and enhancements. Every day the clock is ticking. Be impatient with mediocrity, slow response, and inefficient processes.

◉ **Incent Collaborative Behavior:** *How can you financially incent teams and individuals that support the product, project, or sales team to move fast and be collaborative members of the team?* You will be pleasantly surprised at the performance upgrade that is experienced when there is an *incentive* to deliver by a specific date or time. Incenting behavior quickly fleshes out the top team performers and allows you to move those individuals who are clearly not able to keep up to other roles in the organization where their skill sets may be more effectively utilized.

◉ **Remember That The Clock Is Always Ticking:**
"The clock is always ticking – kick-off is at 3:30 pm Saturday and regardless of all of the delays, roadblocks, equipment problems, access restrictions, and other conflicts, we must deliver at 3:30 pm Saturday. Nobody cares about the issues or reasons things are difficult, or hard, or challenging. They expect kick-off Saturday at 3:30 pm." My good friend Craig is a producer with CBS Sports and recently made this point – one that resounded with me. When the customer sets a date (or date and time in this example), you deliver on or before the date. No excuses acceptable. None. As the leader, you must find ways to clear roadblocks and meet the deliverable date. This requires a sense of urgency and leaves little margin for wasted time.

◉ **Measure, Report, Review:** Establish clear timelines and guardrails for delivery. Report results for specific steps in the overall process. Establish a post-implementation review routine with all members of the organization to ensure that the process is reviewed and necessary changes are made before the next deal hits the funnel. Measurement drives behavior.

BOTTOM LINE

Challenge the process.

EXCEPTIONAL. REMARKABLE.
PHENOMENAL. UNUSUAL.
IMPACTFUL. INCOMPARABLE.
WONDERFUL. NOTABLE. MARVELOUS.
LIMITLESS. FANTASTIC. CURIOUS.
OUTSTANDING. DIFFERENTIATED.
OVER-THE-TOP. UNCOMMON.
SINGULAR. SURPRISING. SPECIAL.
ASTONISHING. RARE. UNIQUE.
UNPRECEDENTED. AMAZING. VIVID.
STRONG. MEMORABLE. INCREDIBLE.
AN ANOMALY.

A DECISION. A CHOICE.
THAT'S EXTRAORDINARY.

CHAPTER 6

BIG IDEA!
METHODS (THE "HOW")
VERSUS RESULTS (THE "WHAT")

"Extraordinary leadership is both hard to define and hard to find.
Extraordinary leaders have a unique ability to both lead and motivate their
teams, all while empowering their people to succeed. It requires a versatile
approach – understanding that every situation is unique and every
individual needs to be led in a different way."

– Steve Rosenstock, Associate Partner, Clarkston Consulting

Your method or process of getting things done is as important, if not more important, than the end result. When you rely on others to accomplish results, the process you use, the actions you take, and the communication style you utilize – all speak of *you*, and therefore your personal brand. Often, up-and-coming leaders fail early in their career due to a lack of focus on the methods they use to drive results. They often leave shattered relationships, broken individuals, burnt-out team members, and an overall bad taste in the mouths of work colleagues.

When you are simply checking boxes and moving so fast that you are running over your team in order to accomplish results, you risk losing their future support.

In the corporate world, this means recognizing that

finance, supply chain, marketing, operations, human resources, and legal teams (to name a few) are there to support you on the project or sales team. They will operate even more effectively *with* you if you treat them with respect and appreciation throughout the process of getting things done. This approach is the only way to get things done in the long-term. In the short-term, investing in relationships that are founded on communication, collaboration, and trust is the best way to ensure that the process moves efficiently. This ensures that hand-offs take place quickly and that there is full alignment on the approach to getting things done. If you burn out your support teams and sever relationships with individuals over one project, don't expect them to be there for you on the next one.

First impressions can make or break a deal. If your expectations for others are all about the results as opposed to the *people* and *process* needed to get there, you will ultimately fail within a large organization. Your actions and behaviors will be remembered and shared with others. And your ultimate career path within an organization may be limited based on how you treat others along the way.

BRINGING IT TO LIFE

◉ **Check Yourself:** The best way to know how you are doing is to ask others. *What would you improve? What would you change? What could you modify to ensure the long-term success of relationships that make* *business happen? Do your team and your support organization feel part of the process – part of your team? Are they actively engaged in meetings, discussions, and working sessions? Do they openly offer their ideas and opinions to you? Are you open to listening? Do others think you are?*

◉ **Celebrate Wins:** The best way to show others how much you appreciate them is to celebrate wins together. Winning fuels momentum. And recognizing great effort is a way to fuel your team and the larger organization. As a leader, recognizing *methods* as wins is as important as recognizing the *achievement* of the end result. If you, as the leader, highlight best practices in process, approach, and methodology, others will understand, recognize, and follow. Highlight extraordinary performance in global communications and messages, detailing the specific business challenge addressed, actions taken, and the qualitative and quantitative results achieved. Recognize extraordinary *support* in a project, pursuit, or initiative. The simple act of publicly recognizing extraordinary performance is an inexpensive method to reward and encourage.

BOTTOM LINE

How you choose to get it done may matter more than what you get done.

EXCEPTIONAL. REMARKABLE.
PHENOMENAL. UNUSUAL.
IMPACTFUL. INCOMPARABLE.
WONDERFUL. NOTABLE. MARVELOUS.
LIMITLESS. FANTASTIC. CURIOUS.
OUTSTANDING. DIFFERENTIATED.
OVER-THE-TOP. UNCOMMON.
SINGULAR. SURPRISING. SPECIAL.
ASTONISHING. RARE. UNIQUE.
UNPRECEDENTED. AMAZING. VIVID.
STRONG. MEMORABLE. INCREDIBLE.
AN ANOMALY.

**A DECISION. A CHOICE.
THAT'S EXTRAORDINARY.**

CHAPTER 7

BIG IDEA!
PRIORITIZE

"Extraordinary leadership is learned behavior. Despite the conventional thinking on this topic, leaders are made, not born. They must be trained, educated, and empowered to face the challenges that lead to progress."

– Gary May, Dean, College of Engineering, Georgia Tech

When I take on too much, I often accomplish less. The challenge is knowing when to say yes, and when to say no. I often find myself falling into the "taking on too much" trap. It is easy to multi-task while leading conference calls, conducting one-on-one meetings, and leading operational working sessions. The end result is I end up giving less than 100% of my focus to participants on a call and/or less than 100% of my focus to discussion topics in meetings. No one wins and my work product is anything but extraordinary.

As a leader, you must sift through the many things that demand your time. You must discern not only the things that *need* to be done, but also the things that *do not* need to be done. Identify and delegate the things that can be done by others. As you delegate tasks, activities, projects, and responsibilities to others, you empower the team to impart their knowledge and expertise and to demonstrate their ability to get things done. As the leader, you will *not* be great at everything. The reality is that when you *try* to be great at everything, you are great at nothing. Your fully exploited strengths and abilities are those things needed by the business to generate results. It takes a great deal of *self-awareness* and *humility* to recognize that others with whom you work bring skills, knowledge, and ability to the team that may far exceed your own.

From a team development perspective, there is a finite amount of time in a day, week, month, or year to provide in-depth coaching, mentoring, and development to individuals. In addition to the team, many high-octane leaders are asked by others inside and outside the organization to be a mentor or coach. This is flattering and, at the same time, can be a source of stress. There is limited time to spend one-on-one with a large number of individuals, especially when balancing your own business and personal priorities. As your career progresses, there is even less time to coach, mentor, and guide others in a unique fashion. *How do you continue to find the time to impact individuals, without losing focus on your own professional and personal priorities?*

The reality is that most of us are in the people business. It is very easy to get caught up in the next meeting, the next customer presentation, the next sales pitch, the next performance review, and the next top-to-top meeting. However, we must take time out to coach and mentor others. We must find time and, in a finite way, invest in the careers of others so that we are making a positive difference with others seeking to pursue extraordinary.

It takes a great deal of self-awareness to recognize when you are spreading yourself too thin across competing priorities. The reality is that it is just not possible to carve out and spend time with everyone that is looking for a career mentor or coach. Instead of saying *no* to everyone, find time to say *yes* to just a few people in a way that allows you to stay true to your personal and professional values, beliefs, and responsibilities while still helping others.

BRINGING IT TO LIFE

- **Test Yourself:** *How many requests of your time do you receive in a given week? How do you prioritize . . . or do you even prioritize? How do you decide where to invest your time and talents as a leader, while saying "no" to other requests in a way that does not burn a relationship bridge?*

- **Focus On The Right Things For You:** I love jumping into the details of day-to-day activities, even when the ball is not being dropped. That's because I feel I can make an impact and drive change quickly. The reality is that, when I do this, I am giving my organization permission to *not* own these responsibilities. Furthermore, they have no opportunity to learn if I am always doing their work. The *less* I jump into day-to-day process details, the *more* I allow individual contributors to accomplish. And, of course, that frees me up to focus on strategic issues and clearing roadblocks to my organization's progress. By doing my team's job for them, I am essentially taking away the opportunity for them to learn, grow, and succeed. *If you were to set up a model, allocating your salary to different activities you are involved with on a daily basis, which activities would "cost" the most? What are the things you are able to easily accomplish, yet are challenging, difficult, or impossible to others? What parts of your job energize, charge, fuel, or motivate you to achieve the extraordinary? What do you wish you could stop doing? If you could free up time in your schedule today, what would you most likely eliminate? Which activities consume the majority of your time? Are these activities that only you can do or that can they be owned by members of your team?*

◉ **Recognize And Delegate:** Your weakness may be another team member's strength. Divide the work to take full advantage of team competencies. Start by recognizing the strengths and weaknesses of your team. Where possible, delegate efforts that sit squarely on your weaknesses and lean into *your* strong skill areas. As a leader building a team, you should be looking to bring together a balanced team that offers multiple strengths to create a collaborative organization. *What is on your plate right now that should be delegated to someone else?*

◎ **Make It Tactical:** When providing career development advice to others, it is just as important to think about the big picture as it is to be aware of the tactical considerations. I recently asked one of my team members what he would like to do next in his career. He outlined for me what he would absolutely love to be doing. As I listened, I immediately went into ideation mode, thinking about all of the possible next steps for this individual. I thought of contacts that could be made on his behalf, skill sets that he has today that would make him a valued resource to a new team, and skills that he should develop to prepare for the next move. We had only worked together for a few months, but my natural instinct was to tactically think about what would be an ideal opportunity for him, even as he was performing in a positive, value-added way on his current team. Understanding the tactical details help when matching people and capabilities to strategic projects and initiatives. *Do you know what an ideal next step role would be for someone you are leading? Are you helping to prepare them for it, even though the timing may not be quite right?*

◎ **Fairness Is Not A Strategy:** "That's not fair!" Like you, I've heard this comment from many a child and even a few business colleagues. Life is not fair. There is no way that a leader can treat everyone equally. Fairness is not a leadership strategy. Some leaders bail out on doing anything for anyone because they fear that it is not fair to do for just one what they wish they could do for everyone. The reality is that the best leaders don't treat everyone equally, but rather differentiate based on individual needs. Demonstrate your passion or desire to make an impact with just a few individuals in spite of wishing you could do the same for all. *If everyone would do for one or a few what they wish they could do for all, can you imagine the impact it would have on the overall organization?*

◉ **Long-Term, In-Depth:** An extraordinary coach or mentor *prioritizes* the coachee in their schedule. They engage for the *long-term*, and value *in-depth* knowledge and understanding of the individual. Don't become the kind of person who claims that they are coaching or mentoring others, and yet cannot tell you anything about their coachees beyond what they are doing in their current role. Clearly, these people have not invested in the individual. *Are you engaged with the people you are coaching? Is it evident from the time you spend with them and your knowledge of them?*

BOTTOM LINE
Doing everything results in doing nothing.

CHAPTER 8

BIG IDEA!
DELIVER RESULTS

---

*"The best a great manager can do is get you to execute
at 100% of your potential. An extraordinary leader gets you to
execute well beyond anything that you thought was possible – well beyond
100%. An extraordinary leader influences by adding value rather
than by relying on title or position."*
– Stephen Brobst, Chief Technology Officer, Teradata

I love college football and am a loyal fan, supporter, and follower. Most seasons, my teams have a winning record and, occasionally, even make a top-tier bowl game! At the same time, they occasionally fail to *complete the play.*

For example, the first season that Georgia Tech played Florida State, GT was up for more than three quarters and poised to win against FSU. Coach Bobby Bowden, moved Charlie Ward into the shotgun formation and suddenly FSU was unstoppable. GT lost. They were not prepared for a switch – a new look or change – in FSU's offensive scheme.

In 2011 GT started out 6-0, and expectations in the GT community were sky high. The team then proceeded to lose five of their last seven games. Again, they failed to adjust. As in any other aspect of life, a loss is a loss regardless of the effort that went into preparation, planning, and execution. If you don't complete the play or deliver results, it's a loss.

So is the case with your personal brand. If you take on a project then drop the ball in execution, you didn't complete the play. If you offer to coach and mentor an individual, yet never make time to meet, discuss, challenge, and provide feedback, you didn't complete the play. If you work many hours, but fail to finish the project or make the number, you didn't complete the play. If you deliver the proposal or contract *after* the due date, you didn't complete the play.

Effort is a baseline expectation. Extraordinary performers find a way to complete the play. Some define personal branding (or the value of your personal brand) through the lens of three criteria: *performance, image*, and *exposure*. When you think of personal branding through this lens, you may have a great image and opportunity for great exposure. But if you lack the business results – your measurable performance results – then your brand value decreases.

Let's revisit the college football analogy. A team may have multiple opportunities to play on ESPN, CBS, or ABC. This is *exposure*. A team may have star players with strong athletic abilities, stellar academic successes, visible morals and values, and may look great in the best Under Armour uniforms available. This is *image*. But over time, a team's poor *performance* on the field will drive away fans, the loss of sponsorship dollars, and trigger negative organization and team momentum. This is the impact of performance and of failing to complete the play.

The same is true in the leadership environment. You may be well known within the organization, involved in multiple facets of the culture, and well-connected relationally. You may have many opportunities to present to fellow executives, other team members, and publicly represent your organization. You may know many people and be known by many others. You may have a positive image and great exposure. And yet, if you repeatedly fail to perform, if you fail to deliver positive business results, then your career within the business may stall or be short lived.

BRINGING IT TO LIFE

◙ **At Work:** *Are you known for delivering results? Do you create performance objectives that are easy to check off, but fail to impact the bottom line? Do you raise your hand to take on new tasks, projects, and responsibilities? Do you challenge the status quo in the pursuit of extraordinary results? Do you raise the bar for your team? Or do you run from challenges or difficult situations? Do you look to make the next job change (or run from your existing role) before dealing with a tough customer or business situation? Do you dump problems on your boss or another team member to address and resolve or do you own it?*

◎ **At Home:** *Are you completing the play in your personal relationships? Are you following through on your commitments to your friends and your family? Would your family say the same? Are you treating them with respect and serving as a role model? Are you investing in family activities and priorities?*

◎ **In The Community:** *Do you show up? Or are you just an inactive member? Do you offer to lead, chair, or facilitate? Do you take on responsibilities that will help and deliver benefits to the community at large? Would the community be thankful for your efforts and follow-through?*

BOTTOM LINE

It's not where you start that's important,
it's where you finish.

CHAPTER 9

BIG IDEA!
PERSISTENCE, PASSION OVER POLITICS, PASSIVITY

"Extraordinary leadership is the ability to generate a 'personal best' effort from every member of the organization. Not through coercion, but through everyone's voluntary commitment to excellence. Extraordinary leadership sustains remarkable results consistently year round, not just during 'Employee Recognition Week.' The extraordinary leader directs and supports others through empathy, enthusiasm, and example."

– Dr. Bill Lampton, Communication Consultant and Speech Coach

---

Have you ever worked for a boss who has felt threatened by you as a team member? Have your performance, contribution, leadership, and passion for making things happen surpassed those of your boss? Most people find themselves in this situation at some point in their career.

Great leaders want to hire great performers. They want to be surrounded by people who are *better* than themselves. They aren't afraid of hiring people who will ultimately be given greater runway within the organization. The challenge for you as a leader is navigating the politics of relationships within an organization. Especially when you naturally raise the bar while others struggle to hold it off the ground.

As we discussed earlier in the book, high-octane performers tend to be pioneers. They challenge the status quo and system thinking. They build relationships and look to build up others along the way. They coach. They mentor. They are naturally able to balance it all and seldom drop any of the proverbial balls. They do not accept mediocre performance. They make decisions faster, often with fewer facts, and are able to *course correct* as needed. They push the envelope or the process. They love to find answers or solutions and refuse to accept *no* or *it's not possible* as an answer. They break the mold, create a new one, and then educate others on how to leverage it. They are impatient with inefficiency, slowness, and those who seek to *put in their hours* versus *committing to achieve something greater.* They are not content with small gains, but would rather use these as momentum as they attack and pursue the greatest of uncharted possibilities. They not only raise the bar, but also define an entirely new level to which the bar should be raised. In a nutshell, high-octane performers pursue persistence and passion over politics and passivity.

My father flew medical helicopters (MEDEVAC) in the Vietnam War (and he has some incredible Jerry Bruckheimer/Michael Bay—worthy stories!). On May 31, 1969, he left the military and started his Hospital Administration Residency at Baptist Hospital in Pensacola, Florida. His Master's thesis was entitled, *Designing Hospital-based Heliports,* and was based on his up-close, personal, and in-depth knowledge of flying numerous life-saving sorties in Vietnam. He wanted to introduce the concept to civilian hospitals starting with Baptist Hospital. Baptist reviewed my father's proposal and the CEO made the executive decision to become the first licensed rooftop and ground based hospital heliport in the state of Florida. Baptist redefined how to use medical helicopters and how to make it financially feasible for patient care in civilian hospitals. This program opened the door to others nationwide in evaluating similar programs.

The decision to present this proposal to Baptist Hospital was pioneering by my father. The decision to agree to invest in the program was pioneering by Baptist and its CEO. If neither had happened, thousands of lives would have been lost as patients would not have reached medical care within the *golden hour* after injury. No doubt other helicopter air ambulance programs would have eventually developed. But when? And after how many additional lives were lost?

High-octane performers pursue greatness, expect the extraordinary, and don't let others stop them from imagining or realizing the possibilities.

BRINGING IT TO LIFE

◙ **Don't Let Anybody Steal Your Joy:** There will be tough days, but not because of work or customer demands, or an endless stream of emails hitting your inbox. They will be tough because there will be times when your friends, colleagues, peers, managers, and leaders take shots at you;

intentionally overlook you; do not support you; disregard a request because they may be afraid you will somehow come out stronger, better, higher, and larger than they are. A high-octane performer will rise above it and let it roll off their shoulders. They will focus on the positive and not allow others to steal their joy or ruin their happiness. They see the world in a completely different way and do not allow others to move them off course.

◉ **Accept And Appreciate Feedback:** Sometimes your tendency may be to ignore feedback. Instead, seek it out, accept it, and appreciate it. Note your lessons learned, for better or worse. Aggressively act on what you hear and resolve to use it as fuel toward a stronger future. Feedback can be a gift. The key to winning with others is to first accept and acknowledge, then outline a plan to act on it. If you ignore it, you will fuel a perception of arrogance. And that perception does not serve a persistent and passionate leader well.

◉ **Be Persistent:** As you can imagine, translating the Baptist Hospital Life Flight program concept into reality required a significant amount of persistence, determination, and investment of time to develop the business plan and gain alignment with key executives. Nothing would have been accomplished if persistence and passion had been lacking. Plus many lives would have been lost. This also holds true for you. You must find your passions and be persistent with your ideas and concepts. Press on!

BOTTOM LINE
Persistence pays off.

EXCEPTIONAL. REMARKABLE.
PHENOMENAL. UNUSUAL.
IMPACTFUL. INCOMPARABLE.
WONDERFUL. NOTABLE. MARVELOUS.
LIMITLESS. FANTASTIC. CURIOUS.
OUTSTANDING. DIFFERENTIATED.
OVER-THE-TOP. UNCOMMON.
SINGULAR. SURPRISING. SPECIAL.
ASTONISHING. RARE. UNIQUE.
UNPRECEDENTED. AMAZING. VIVID.
STRONG. MEMORABLE. INCREDIBLE.
AN ANOMALY.

**A DECISION. A CHOICE.
THAT'S EXTRAORDINARY.**

CHAPTER 10

BIG IDEA!
BE BOLD ... JUST ASK

"Extraordinary leaders instill commitment versus compliance.
Listen for possibilities. Speak for things. Understand that clarity is
power. Seek an environment of active mutual support (versus peaceful
co-existence). Extraordinary leaders challenge the process,
inspire a shared vision, enable others to act, model the right way
to treat others, and celebrate the heart!"

– Rick Brindle, Vice President,
eSales and Industry Development, Kraft Foods

When I first started work at Coca-Cola Enterprises, I read an article about the culture, the people, and the history of the company. One of the key figures profiled was Don Keough who had served as President and COO of the Coca-Cola Company. He was instrumental in the establishment of Coca-Cola Enterprises and was a leader on numerous philanthropic and educational boards. It was obvious that he was investing in people within the business and in the community. A colleague of mine suggested that I reach out to him as I was interested in not only knowing more about the business, but also how he was able to effectively balance his leadership in the business with engagement in personal and philanthropic endeavors. I wrote him a note and within two weeks his assistant called me to schedule a meeting. I asked. He accepted.

We decided to meet at his Atlanta office and, I must say, I was relatively unprepared for the meeting. While I had done my homework on Mr. Keough, I really did not grasp the enormity of his knowledge, relationships, and general presence. At the same time, perhaps that is what made the meeting so special.

Upon entering his office, I was greeted by numerous photos and memorabilia featuring Mr. Keough with some of the world's best known leaders. On his desk sat my handwritten note, several enclosures I had sent, and a few notes he had scribbled together. He asked, "Tell me again, why are you here?" Without hesitation, I outlined a number of business questions I had prepared prior to our meeting. I also asked him about his career path and any lessons learned he could share with me based on my career stage, role, and background. That opened the door and the conversation progressed. He appreciated my openness and interest in learning. He provided insights on how the Coca-Cola System was organized and he shared his life lessons from time on the leadership team at Coca-Cola and as a board member. It was a great conversation – and I took copious notes.

My first lesson was that busy people can always make time for discussions and meetings that they deem important. Mr. Keough had a full calendar, yet he made time to fit me into his schedule (see earlier chapters for references on the "Do For One" concept – this was certainly an example). My second lesson was that I validated the value of asking great questions. I am naturally inquisitive and truly enjoyed asking him as many questions as I could fit into the brief time we had together. He did the talking – which was my intent. And I listened and learned. Lastly, he gave me several great pointers to consider in navigating the intricacies of a large global organization.

BRINGING IT TO LIFE

◉ **Just Ask:** If I had never written the note, I would never have gotten the meeting. If I had never made an effort, no effort would have been offered in return. If you don't ask for the meeting, the discussion, the conversation or the conference call, you will never get it. *Are you asking?*

◉ **Develop The Art Of Asking Extraordinary Questions:** Not only from this meeting, but from my interactions with other peers, colleagues, and executives, I have learned the value of asking great questions. Asking questions is good. Asking insightful, meaningful, inquisitive, and interesting questions is extraordinary. This is more art than skill. A question asked without emotion may generate a response devoid of emotion. But great questions, asked with great interest, empathy, and appreciation, can generate extraordinary conversation and knowledge transfer. Asking questions is an alternative method of engaging and participating in dialogue and conversation *before* offering an opinion or idea.

◉ **Accept Every Opportunity To Speak:** One piece of advice Mr. Keough offered readily was to immediately, and without question, accept, embrace, and learn from every opportunity to share knowledge, experiences, ideas, and inspirations with groups. Accept every opportunity to speak that fits within your schedule.

BOTTOM LINE
Just ask. The answer might be "Yes!"

CHAPTER 11

BIG IDEA!
THE ART OF SELF-PROMOTION

"Extraordinary leadership is being inclusive and knowing
that every decision will have positive and negative repercussions.
A true leader is one that can rise above all the chatter and distracting
dialogue/rhetoric, recognize that in reality there is no true 'win-win,'
and can see which combination of positive and negative outcomes
will have the greatest impact on the largest population. Extraordinary
leaders often do not make popular decisions, because they operate
with greater awareness and do what is truly needed."

– Ravi Naidu, Technology Executive; Actor and Comedian

Ambitious[1] <adj>: *Having or showing a strong
desire and determination to succeed. Intended
to satisfy high aspirations and therefore difficult
to achieve.*

Tenacious[2] <adj>: *Not easily dispelled or
discouraged; persisting in existence or in a course
of action.*

*What does self-promotion mean to you? Is it a topic
with which you are familiar, comfortable and passionate
about?* It means ensuring that your manager is aware
of your accomplishments. It means seeking feedback
and credit, where appropriate. It means proactively
networking with influential figures inside and/or

outside of the business. It means ensuring that others on your team are recognized upward and across, and that *their* accomplishments are celebrated. When they win, you win.

Self-promotion demonstrates that you are ready for the next challenge or, at a minimum, have a desire to take on additional responsibilities. Self-promotion is your outward demonstration of self-confidence. It is also you demonstrating a vision for the future – a desire to make a difference. It is balancing confidence and assertiveness with professionalism and personality.

The result is that others take notice. Others come to know you, your interests, and your passions. Others are invited to buy into your brand. You are top of mind. And others are interested because *you* are interesting.

The challenge with self-promotion is that it sounds and feels unnatural. The key is making it part of your routine in a tactful, relevant way. It starts with knowing your audience. For example, when I make strides in my personal pursuits outside of work (music, writing, speaking, etc.), I share these accomplishments with a small subset of my total network. These are individuals that appreciate my passion for these interests and recognize them for the value they bring to others. Some in my network that do not know me well might perceive this information as being boastful or arrogant. Therefore, I do not include them on my list for these updates and communications.

The same thinking may be employed at work.

CHAPTER 11 – THE ART OF SELF-PROMOTION

What you accomplish at work and what your team accomplishes together may be perfectly appropriate to celebrate and communicate to company colleagues and associates but completely inappropriate for Facebook and LinkedIn colleagues. Organizational leaders love to recognize and celebrate wins, especially over the competition! When we sign the next multi-year contract, my business colleagues will appreciate and celebrate the win. But to someone working in another business altogether, with no context of the accomplishment, it is a wasted communication.

Saying less is saying more. If you are on Facebook, you inevitably have friends who post status updates covering every aspect of their lives. At some point you tune them out or un-friend them. Whether at work or outside of work, what you say and how frequently you communicate correlates directly to others' interest in listening to you.

By using facts and figures, you are able to take the focus off of you and center the message on the accomplishment of results. When I communicate major team accomplishments at work, I mix numbers with relational and personal recognition. I am also selective about frequency of messaging, sometimes saving news to bundle into a larger communication.

I was recently at breakfast with a colleague who is an up-and-coming leader within another business where I volunteer my time. We had begun a conversation on self-promotion and as we sat down, he asked, "How do I make others aware of my desire to do more, to step up, and to take on more responsibility, without it appearing to be an overt strategy to 'take over' or 'one-up' others?"

Great question! Essentially, he wanted to know how to self-promote without appearing overly confident, competitive, or boastful. I asked him who he admired within his organization. I asked who he would most like to receive coaching and advice from if the opportunity presented itself. I asked who he could reach out to and engage as members of his personal advisory board. We then discussed a list of questions that he could ask that would demonstrate his knowledge of the organization, his interest in the long-term vision, his passion for the mission, and his overwhelming desire to be a part of leading and growing the organization in the future. These *questions* serve as his mechanism for *artful self-promotion*. He was able to express his interest in doing more while subtly explaining that he feels like his capacity is greater than his current demands. *Who owns your career? If not you, who?*

BRINGING IT TO LIFE

◉ **Communicate Up:** *Does your boss or manager know what you are truly passionate about? Does she know your true strengths? Does he understand the vision you have for your career?*

◉ **Communicate Out:** *How much time during the week do you dedicate to professional development? How* *much time do you spend building relationships outside of your current team, meeting with leaders in other parts of the business, or meeting with colleagues in other parts of the business altogether? How much time are you investing in developing your intra-company network?* These are all relationships that might provide some bit of insight, advice, or counsel that could prove useful in your career progression. *If you don't reach out, how will other leaders know you? How do you ensure that the "full schedule" does not stop you from investing strategically in new relationships?*

◉ **Coach The Team:** *How do you assist your team with self-promotion?* First, when someone new joins my team, I provide him or her with a lengthy list of organization leaders with whom to meet – individuals that support our team and who are also making a significant impact in the organization. I want to immediately kick-start their internal company network. I encourage the new person to make it a point to meet everyone on this list at some point in their first 90-120 days on the job. *What steps are you taking to assist your team in developing their reach within the organization, thereby establishing a platform for their own self-promotion now and in the future?*

◉ **Think Beyond The HR Process:** Most talent management processes are structured to provide visibility into talent within a *specific* business group. The formalized process may include regular talent roundtables at which people leaders present their team, recognize top performers, and help place talent in open boxes on the organization chart. It may also include formal talent mapping and tagging. The challenge with these structured talent processes is that they typically *do not* cross over into other organization segments. For example, if you are in supply chain and your aspiration is to work in strategic brand management or sales, you are most likely not even going to show up on the talent management *snapshot* reviewed by leadership in that part of the organization. The only solution is for you to invest in developing relationships with leaders in that part of the business so that you can learn more about their organization, understand the types of skills and abilities needed in specific roles, and educate them on your passions, your strengths, and your value proposition. This is all part of active and effective self-promotion.

◉ **Accept And Appreciate Support:** Accept others who choose to help you with your own self-promotion. When you are recognized, appreciate it. Wins do not come often enough for most, and many are not recognized publicly. When given the opportunity, take it and appreciate it. And pay it forward. If the opportunity exists, identify the other individuals who played a part in your win. Celebrating others is a great leadership character trait and will strengthen your brand.

BOTTOM LINE

If it's to be, it must be me.

EXCEPTIONAL. REMARKABLE.
PHENOMENAL. UNUSUAL.
IMPACTFUL. INCOMPARABLE.
WONDERFUL. NOTABLE. MARVELOUS.
LIMITLESS. FANTASTIC. CURIOUS.
OUTSTANDING. DIFFERENTIATED.
OVER-THE-TOP. UNCOMMON.
SINGULAR. SURPRISING. SPECIAL.
ASTONISHING. RARE. UNIQUE.
UNPRECEDENTED. AMAZING. VIVID.
STRONG. MEMORABLE. INCREDIBLE.
AN ANOMALY.

A DECISION. A CHOICE.
THAT'S EXTRAORDINARY.

CHAPTER 12

BIG IDEA!
BE INTERESTING

"Extraordinary leadership is focusing on the team and each team member, while projecting a sincere, pure, positive, and happy picture. It is believing in the vision and spirit of the mission."

– Lola Dee, Concierge; Singer; Songwriter;
World-renowned Performer and Entertainer

I speak regularly with groups on various subjects, including leadership, personal branding, life balance, navigating change, and one of my favorite subjects, pursuing passions in life.

Inevitably, when my presentation is complete, I have a handful of individuals tell me, "I have always thought about doing XYZ, but I never took the steps to do it."

For example, "I have always thought about writing a book." - "I have always wanted to learn to play the guitar." - "I have always thought about going on a mission trip to a foreign country." - "I have always thought about taking acting lessons." Sadly, these people never made the time or did the homework to figure out what to do first. They never took a risk and never stopped making excuses.

Remember when we were young: growing up through high school and college, and everything seemed possible? There was little to worry about. We had minimal personal responsibility and plenty of time for sports, music, choir, gymnastics, dance, art, and every other extra-curricular activity imaginable. But as we get older, life seems to take on added complexity and it forces us out of our *creative* zone and into a *routine* zone. The days become shorter and the hours seem to fly by. There are many priorities and most take precedence over our personal desires, interests, or hobbies. We forsake creative talents because of a lack of perceived time and resources.

Whether you recognize it or not, we are all born with personal talents and gifts. Some are small. Some are large. Some are obvious. Others are more subtle. All are significant. Many are ignored or go unused.

I wrote my first song when I was 32 years old. I was way over the hill by most music industry standards! But I will never forget the emotional impact of that first song. It was called "Shadow of the Blade" and I based it on my father's stories of flying MEDEVAC helicopters as an Army pilot in Vietnam. I wrote the lyrics and melody and went into a small studio in Atlanta to add drum and guitar parts. When I played it for my dad he broke down in tears. Seeing that emotional impact from something I wrote was amazing. I was shocked. Then interested and excited to write more.

I began writing country music and wrote the title

track for my first album, *Saturday in the South*, while tailgating at a Georgia Tech college football game. The song captures the essence of college football game-day. Perseverance paid off. Several years after releasing the first version of the song, I met Alex, a leader in the country music industry in Nashville. He loved the song and suggested we make a few modifications. The revised version was picked up by Grammy Award winner and country music superstar, Tracy Lawrence, who re-recorded it and released it. That version was then picked up by CBS Sports and Fox Sports to be used as part of their national college football broadcasts.

Many people initially laughed at my endeavor to write, sing, and produce music. But that's exactly what I did. I went on to release a second album of contemporary Christian music called, *Let Go & Let God*, and have since written numerous singles spanning the country, Christian, and pop genres. It's fun. It's interesting. It's a passion.

That passion can be contagious! Several years ago, I arrived at the office when one of my colleagues walked into my office and made this energetic statement: "I'm a whole new Heather!" Several weeks prior, Heather had decided to find time to start taking voice lessons. She had an immediate connection with her voice coach, and through that relationship, she was asked to join a performing group; all within a matter of a few weeks! Heather was thrilled, and this wasn't about quitting her day job. It was about finding an outlet for her passion in music and being able to quickly leverage it into performance and entertainment. Heather asked me, "Why did I wait so long?" as she bounded out of the office to her first meeting of the day.

Another friend, also in his late 30's, started taking acting lessons. He appeared in several commercials and will soon be featured in a major blockbuster movie. He didn't need to quit his day job working for one of the largest technology companies. This is his hobby.

Yet another friend, who is in her early 40's, works in leadership development by day. She found time to pursue her passion in writing and authored a book about relationship challenges which has positively impacted many people around the world who are struggling with divorce.

The biggest failure of adults is the failure to *stay curious. What story will you tell one day?*

BRINGING IT TO LIFE

◉ **Define It:** *What is it that you would like to make time for in life? Exercise? Reading? Writing? Singing? Performing? Traveling? Masters swimming? Competitive tennis? Playing an instrument?* Start by writing it down, and make sure it is well defined. Talk to others that have done it. Learn the process, the pitfalls, and how to make it work for you.

◉ **Make Connections:** I*s there anyone you know who is doing something similar, and may be able to provide coaching or feedback on getting started and making* *it happen?* In my case, I found an article in the *Atlanta Business Chronicle* that profiled an executive in town who was writing, singing, and performing country music. I reached out to him one afternoon and we met the next day. We hit it off and soon after our initial meeting, he introduced me to his voice coach, Heidi (who I still work with today). It was Heidi who encouraged me to start writing songs and explore recording. Today, music is part of my life routine. Before I wrote my first book, I interviewed six different authors in my network in order to better understand the process they went through to get published. Your network can be an invaluable asset when it comes to the pursuit of creativity.

◉ **Make Time:** Despite your full calendar, it *is* possible to find time to pursue your passions. It will require some strategic time management and an investment on your part, and on the part of any significant other(s). Like playing the piano or singing in a band, many passions require practice and the investment of time. *Are you ready to make the commitment to share your time with a new hobby or passion?*

◉ **Budget For It:** A hobby does *not* have to be expensive, and starting small is certainly a great approach. You will make mistakes and they will have a cost associated with them. I spent time and money on music promotions and publicity that were a complete waste and generated no results. I simply did not know any better as I was new to the industry. The important thing is to learn from those experiences. *What can you do to set aside time to pursue your passions? What kind of investment do you need to make? Can you budget margin into your life as well, so you can at least say you tried?* No regrets!

◉ **Celebrate It:** Self-promotion is not natural. Nor is it easy as we discussed in the previous chapter. It is required for creative products that you are looking to commercialize. It's a catch-22. Many people will truly enjoy hearing your music, checking out your work, seeing you perform at the comedy club or in a Broadway show, buying your custom-made jewelry, or reading your book. And yet they will not know about it if you do not promote it, celebrate it, and share it. When I release a new song, I talk about it across social media platforms, blog about it, distribute an email newsletter, and more. *Are you prepared to self-promote?* Be bold.

◉ **Focus:** Most importantly, don't let anybody take you off track when you reveal that you are investing in a new hobby. *What's holding you back? What steps can you take to make time for that one passion, that one hobby, or that one interest?* You don't want to look back on your life and say, "If only . . . ." You never know where it might lead. You never know what might happen in life if you are not willing to be open to the possibilities. Either way, enjoy the ride. It's your life … make it interesting! And remember that every day is another chapter in your life story.

BOTTOM LINE

When you are interesting, others are interested!

EXCEPTIONAL. REMARKABLE.
PHENOMENAL. UNUSUAL.
IMPACTFUL. INCOMPARABLE.
WONDERFUL. NOTABLE. MARVELOUS.
LIMITLESS. FANTASTIC. CURIOUS.
OUTSTANDING. DIFFERENTIATED.
OVER-THE-TOP. UNCOMMON.
SINGULAR. SURPRISING. SPECIAL.
ASTONISHING. RARE. UNIQUE.
UNPRECEDENTED. AMAZING. VIVID.
STRONG. MEMORABLE. INCREDIBLE.
AN ANOMALY.

**A DECISION. A CHOICE.
THAT'S EXTRAORDINARY.**

CHAPTER 13

BIG IDEA!
PERSONAL MOMENTUM

"Extraordinary leadership is both inspiring and realistic. In companies, non-profits, and governments, transformative leaders create a vision for the future, share that message with internal and external audiences, articulate the specific steps to take, and affirm each employee, vendor, customer, shareholder, and community leader role in the process. Moreover, extraordinary leaders value the time, energy, experience, and ideas of every member of the organization. This is proven by their willingness to hear the bad news as well as the good."

– Jennifer Hartz, President, Corporate Hartz, LLC

Have you ever found yourself on a roll? Projects are being approved and moving forward. Demand is strong and customers are appreciative. Your partnerships are evolving. You are recognized for your accomplishments. Career growth seems inevitable versus questionable. Your team is performing well. Your personal life is hitting on all cylinders. You feel and see *the wins.* Positive events have created positive momentum.

Conversely, have you ever felt like you just couldn't catch a break? Everyone else seems to be moving forward while you encounter roadblocks. Your career is in neutral or reverse. You've taken a hit, and then another and they just somehow start to pile up. Personal loss compounds with frustration at work. Negative events have reversed positive momentum.

As an individual with your own personal brand, there are times when you have positive momentum carrying you through the ups and downs of life – through the challenging situations and through the difficult circumstances. As the owner of your brand, you must ensure that you recognize these moments and understand what drove their evolution; so you can replicate them in the future. At the same time, when you encounter negative events, negative personal situations, challenges at work, or outside influences that generate negative momentum for your brand, you must use these moments as an opportunity for personal growth. Leverage these as an opportunity to recognize them and learn from them; then pursue the next steps based on what you have learned.

When I experience personal wins, personal recognition, and personal accomplishments, I actually *increase* my efforts to take on and engage in *more*. I leverage these wins as fuel for making an even bigger difference. Conversely, when it seems like walls are crumbling, relationships are strained, and decisions are not resulting in extraordinary outcomes, I take a step back to reassess and learn.

Personal momentum can be positive or negative. It can be triggered by varying circumstances, events, or relationships. As a leader, it is imperative that you recognize the elements in life that drive positive personal momentum so that you may exploit them fully, while minimizing the impact of negative momentum events.

BRINGING IT TO LIFE

◉ **Build:** As a leader, personal momentum may be the ultimate catalyst for your team's growth and achievement. Recognize it. Embrace it. And leverage it fully as fuel to push the team to raise the bar. Energy from positive momentum is contagious, and personal momentum will translate into positive growth for the team and organization. *What are you doing to identify, capture, and build on your personal momentum?*

◉ **Assess:** Leaders make time to step back and assess drivers of personal momentum. It is imperative that you identify what fuels you. *What is it that drives positive forward momentum for you as an individual? Is it rewards and recognition? Is it seeing others achieving greatness due to your coaching and mentoring? Is it delivering results? Is it being asked to take on more? Conversely, what drives negative personal momentum in your life? Is it negative words and opinions from peers and colleagues? Is it failing to achieve results? Is it not being recognized and rewarded when others are center stage? Is it personal loss? Or is it a compounding of multiple roadblocks in life?*

◉ **Persist:** Morgan Freeman shared this statement at a recent business event I attended: "The world will walk right past a person sitting down, but will always reach down to help someone struggling to get up." Simple statement, powerful message.

When you make an effort and fail, it is natural that others want to help you recover, move you forward, and find success. When you give up and do not even make an effort, people aren't as willing to help. *Why should you expect others to care when you don't even care yourself?*

BOTTOM LINE
Personal momentum translates directly into organizational momentum.

CHAPTER 14

BIG IDEA!
A NETWORK OF CONNECTORS

"Extraordinary leadership is the result of three steps – embracing your unique ability to lead; identifying an opportunity where you can make a difference; and finally rallying the right people to make some serious noise. Life's too short to not be noisy."

– Cathy Hotka, CEO, Cathy Hotka & Associates

Do you invest regularly in your network? Are you building relationships with others in the business, philanthropic, and non-profit communities?

Networking isn't merely collecting business cards and filling up your Rolodex. It's more about building a list of contacts with whom one has a limited relational foundation. It is sometimes confused with job searching. Unfortunately, networking can also be construed as fake or self-serving, and may not be about creating a two-way relationship.

Relationship-building, on the other hand, involves investing in individuals at a deeper, more meaningful level. You want to create value beyond the short-term. Meet someone. Get to know them. Then start building a genuine relationship, without any ulterior motive or end-game interest in transacting business with them in the future. This deeper investment in people may eventually lead to a more natural, strong and mutual business relationship.

These relationships fuel professional and personal development. Your network can be a powerful tool in selling new business, rounding out your personal brand, and broadening your awareness of community and political trends and priorities. If you are pursuing a strategic leadership role within your organization, your network can be a powerful tool for getting things done. It is a personal brand asset.

The reality is that many individuals fail to realize that it is wise to have relationships that extend beyond their employer's four walls. Most assumed that the job market would remain strong, as it had for many years during the 1990s. Not many people expected the downturn that resulted in countless jobs being lost. Prior to that, venture capitalists chased every new start-up, while jobs were plentiful. What became apparent after the bubble burst was the value of maintaining invested, long-term relationships outside the four walls of a single employer.

Long-term network partnerships extend well beyond the day-to-day job environment. If you are looking to expand your role within an organization, or even pursue public office, trust-based relationships are absolutely critical to driving change and gaining insight into areas new to your internal knowledge base.

Authenticity is the core value that many lack in

building relationships. I have an acquaintance who regularly invites me and others to breakfasts and lunches, yet he simply comes across as fake, contrived, and unauthentic. His mistake is that he is trying to build a Rolodex and collect a pile of contacts, as opposed to truly investing in building relationships. His approach is always the same. He gives the appearance of being interested in a personal connection and the conversation flows for about 15 minutes. Then he inevitably, and quite clumsily, moves to the *"big ask"* of who he should reach out to at the company to talk to about selling-in consulting services; or who he should send his resume to for a new job. He has good intentions, but he fails in the execution.

Here are a few tips for developing and maintaining a powerful set of relationships.

First, consider *avoiding* stated networking events. *Why invest your time in networking for the sake of networking?!* These events do not typically offer an environment for relationship-development and growth.

Second, ferociously *manifest and invest* in relationships with other *connectors*. These are people with whom you feel you have an immediate connection, and through whom you sense an opportunity to potentially do more together. Look for people who have extensive *reach* and typically have a *circle of influence* that overlaps, but does not mimic, your own. Connectors are fueled by the energy of other connectors, and have a restless desire to do more.

Third, make it part of your routine to regularly meet in person with a subset of your network. Think of it as a rotation. *Face-to-face* is the absolute best method for maintaining and strengthening relationships. Be sure to make time in your schedule to glean perspective from valued members of your personal network.

Fourth, in every possible way, strive to *connect others*. There is no greater satisfaction than seeing two individuals within your network connect, find common ground, and pursue a relationship together that results in mutual benefit.

Fifth, be *protective* of your relationships. I do not immediately bring acquaintances into my network and do not automatically provide them with access to my friends, colleagues, and partners. It is only *after* we have built a relationship of trust, and they have transcended from acquaintance to colleague or friend, that I will introduce them to others in my network. Your network will appreciate this selectiveness and will recognize that, when you introduce someone to them, or suggest that they meet someone, it is important.

Sixth, use *technology* to enable the network. I leverage most of the capabilities of LinkedIn and other social sites in addition to tracking my network with software and portable technology. I make notes on people that I meet. I track contact information as if it were *data gold*. Social media makes it easier for you to make it part of your daily routine to reach out to, and stay engaged with your network.

BRINGING IT TO LIFE

◉ **Build A Routine:** As a leader, you must make relationship management part of your routine. For each person, the process, approach, activities, and actions will differ. You must define what works for you – and then implement it. Your network is an important aspect of your brand value. *What is your networking process or routine?*

◉ **Invest:** First, invest in others. The benefits of investing without expecting anything in return is that you build trust-based relationships. Investing in others builds relationship equity that may be leveraged over time to mutual benefit. *Who do you know that may benefit from meeting others in your network? What can you do to help others get ahead?*

◉ **Prioritize:** One challenge connected and connector people face is how to divide time between friends with expectations. Friends in the software business looking for the next deal (and want to be connected). Friends desiring to leave one company to get a job at another (and want to be connected). Friends looking for tickets to the next hot event or concert (and want to be connected). Friends looking for that one piece of advice, guidance, or introduction that can propel their career to the next level (and want to be connected). And the list goes on. If you are a connector, you understand this completely. The challenge becomes how you manage your time and still maintain quality relationships. *How do you stay focused on priorities and ensure that you do not get lost in everyone else's requests?* The answer is ... you probably can't. It's not fair to everyone in your network or every one of your relationships. But it is reality.

◉ **Connect With Connectors:** Not everyone is a connector. And whether or not you categorize yourself as a connector, your *network of connectors* will be invaluable. You never know when a relationship will yield something of positive benefit. Check your network. *Who do you know that is a true connector? What is your relationship like with that individual? Could it be better? Should it be better? How are you helping this person?*

BOTTOM LINE
People buy from people based
on relationships and trust.

CHAPTER 15

BIG IDEA!
RELATIONSHIPS FUEL PERSONAL BRAND VALUE

"Extraordinary leadership starts with great human values, including a tremendous respect for other people, a strong ability to envision what the future should hold for the organization, and an even stronger skill set to articulate that vision. And of course, an implacable drive to achieve the vision while overcoming obstacles along the journey!"

– Joe Irwin, President and CEO, Georgia Tech Alumni Association

Networking is important. Relationships are key!

People find new jobs or careers through the network of the people they know and have a relationship with. Community organizations successfully raise money because of the people that they develop a relationship with over time. New hobbies or passions can often be pursued because of an existing connection within a relationship.

Thanks to my network, I am able to help others connect quickly in a way that brings value to both sides of the relationship. I can quickly get answers to questions, explore big ideas, and pursue my passions and creative outlets. I am able to explore business partnerships that, in the past, had not been explored.

Your personal brand is strengthened or weakened

based on the value of your personal network and the inherent relationships built into the network. Perhaps due to technology and the ease of social (online) networking, it seems that fewer and fewer individuals are investing in building *true* personal relationships. As a result, the true connectors – those who are genuinely interested in knowing you, knowing others, and connecting you with others for mutual benefit – are the ones that really stand out.

What are you doing to invest in your network? Here are four network circles in which to invest.

Inter-Company Network: *Who do you know within your team that can help you take the ordinary and make it extraordinary? What knowledge is available from other team members that is not currently being exploited? Who do you know outside of your team, but within your organization? How are you helping or bringing them something of value and developing a relationship and/or understanding of their part of the business? What can you learn from other groups within your company or organization? How do they interface with customers or support customer activity? Do they complement or intersect your day-to-day business activities?*

Industry Network: *Are you in the loop with trends, insights, and future forecasts of your industry? Have you connected with others doing similar roles, at similar companies? What are their best practices and how can you potentially apply those in your environment? Are you involved in local, regional, and national industry events to ensure you stay "up to speed" on your industry and the industry of your customers?*

While content sessions are always interesting, the true value comes from developing one-on-one connections with others (peers, colleagues, and potential clients) who are also attending.

Community Network: Oftentimes business relationships are built based upon a shared mutual passion created while working on non-business, community, or philanthropic endeavors. By getting involved, you inherently begin to establish a network with leaders that most likely are outside your current day-to-day operating circle. *Are you lending your leadership talents to organizations outside the walls of your current job? Are you involved in your community on a larger level? Does giving back mean giving of your time and talents, and not simply writing a check?*

Social Network: Social networks have exploded over the years. Invest in them, engage in them, and determine how you can leverage them to your benefit. For example, use LinkedIn to learn about individuals with whom you may be partnering. Use Facebook to connect with friends, both old and new. Use Twitter to pull news, follow organizations, and keep in touch with individuals. Share your interests via Pinterest to learn more about the interests and activities of your network. While social networks can't take the place of traditional relationship-building, they should become a part of your overall networking vocabulary and something for which you need to make time. These social interaction tools and systems will very quickly evolve and change.

As a leader plugged into society, stay social. Recognize that younger generations of workers are engaging socially naturally as they have been raised surrounded by smartphones and social media platforms.

BRINGING IT TO LIFE

◉ **Create A "Network" Strategy:** *What is your routine for keeping in touch with individuals with whom you meet? How are you connecting with others inside and outside of the company? What value are you bringing to them and what are you learning? How do you keep track of the contact information of new people that you meet?* Develop a strategy that works for you and know that everyone has a different method for maintaining relationships. What you create will be uniquely yours.

◉ **Filter:** You cannot invest in everyone. Recognize that you cannot connect over coffee, breakfast, or lunch with everyone you meet. You cannot expand and exploit every potential new relationship. You must be judicious with the use of your time, so as not to get distracted from your primary day-to-day business objectives. Your filter will get stronger over time as you have the opportunity to spend time with the right and wrong people. The ability to filter requests is a key aspect of prioritization and managing your time, which links directly to the prioritization topic we covered earlier in the book.

◉ **Deliver Extraordinary Follow-Up:** Be the best at *follow-up*. Regardless of whether or not you have an interest or even the time, always respond to calls and emails. Write thank you emails and handwritten thank you notes to individuals that you meet. You never know when an individual will resurface in your network, and may be in a position to help you out. Because so many people do not follow-up with a handwritten note, your follow-up will be memorable. Extraordinary means being different, unique, personal, engaged, and fast.

◉ **Offer Unexpected Value:** When you connect with friends or business colleagues, think through what you can do for that individual before you even get together. *To whom can you introduce them? Who should they meet? What article or book did you read that would be beneficial to pass along? Where can you work together to help others?* When you think of others first, you will ultimately benefit.

◉ **Build Your Network By Helping Others:** Pass on job leads, share best practices, or mutual mentoring for success. By helping others, they will help you. Be a *connector*. The adage, *pay it forward* absolutely works.

◉ **Employ Routines To Stay Connected:** Set aside time each week for staying in touch with your network. Utilize email, phone calls, and social media messages to stay connected and to connect others. The key is to develop a routine that allows you to rotate through your contacts and to invest time where it is worth investing. Note that *not every contact* is worth keeping on the list and, over time, you will learn to filter your network appropriately.

◉ **Drive Network Growth:** Participation in community and philanthropic endeavors is a great way to meet new people, develop new relationships, and expand your reach. In addition, there are excellent leadership development opportunities that arise from engaging in community organizations. Many business professionals have been recruited or hired into a new job by virtue of their community connections.

◉ **Ask For Advice:** Since advisors and mentors have typically "been there, done that" they can offer great advice on building and maintaining productive relationships. One word of caution: keep in mind that your life is your life, and while mentors provide advice and opinions, it is your responsibility to own your decisions and consequences. They are not life experts on what will work for you.

◉ **Recognize And Appreciate Personality Differences:** Some people are natural people persons, while others tend to be a bit more quiet or introverted. It is important to know when to *dial it up* or *dial it down*; and how to adjust your style to those with whom you meet. Just as much as high energy can be a major turnoff to some, so can low energy. Keep in mind that the best relationships are often built when one appreciates the ideas, opinions, behaviors, and preferences of others.

◉ **Rate It:** *On a scale of 1 to 10, how would you rate your network?*

BOTTOM LINE

It's not the network, it's your network!

EXCEPTIONAL. REMARKABLE.
PHENOMENAL. UNUSUAL.
IMPACTFUL. INCOMPARABLE.
WONDERFUL. NOTABLE. MARVELOUS.
LIMITLESS. FANTASTIC. CURIOUS.
OUTSTANDING. DIFFERENTIATED.
OVER-THE-TOP. UNCOMMON.
SINGULAR. SURPRISING. SPECIAL.
ASTONISHING. RARE. UNIQUE.
UNPRECEDENTED. AMAZING. VIVID.
STRONG. MEMORABLE. INCREDIBLE.
AN ANOMALY.

A DECISION. A CHOICE.
THAT'S EXTRAORDINARY.

CHAPTER 16

BIG IDEA!
ALWAYS ON

"Successful businesses are no different than successful
families raising children. You must create an environment for the
child to flourish and grow, which is true of corporations that
have the vision to look beyond this quarter's earnings. So, in a nutshell,
this was my epiphany … extraordinary leaders lead with the heart of a
parent, the wisdom of a favorite teacher, the motivation of a challenging
coach, and the inspiration of an evangelist."

– Jack Spartz, Regional Vice President, BI Worldwide

Building a business and building effective partnerships can be a 24-hour job. It is part of your daily life fabric. And every interaction – planned and unplanned – is an opportunity to meet that next buyer, influencer, or business partner.

I recently attended a business event in Washington, D.C. This event had nothing to do with my current business. In fact it was an event I was attending with my wife. While at the reception, we began talking with a woman neither one of us knew. The adage "it's a small world" held true, and we were soon discussing our many professional connections. She used to work with one of my top prospects and she knew all the buyers with whom we were now engaged. You just never know where you might meet that next influencer or decision-maker. Business development is not just making cold calls or attending customer partnership meetings. Rather, it continues at industry events, leadership events, and in the community. Every interaction, speech, or presentation is an opportunity to represent you and your company's brand, and could yield a relationship of mutual benefit.

Most industries are also small communities. When I worked in management consulting, I worked with teams of absolute rock-star, A-player, make-things-happen, high-octane performers. Today those individuals are dispersed across numerous businesses and organizations and serve as great references in their industry. I utilize these relationships to better understand current business situations, key priorities, and primary decision makers within prospect organizations; and they do the same. I always make time for them when they are looking to map a strategy for working with my organization.

The concept of *it's a small world* is alive and well in business today. Within certain industries, you will find that everybody knows everybody – or knows somebody that knows everybody. This can be powerful when leveraged correctly. This comes to life when you ask colleagues within an existing customer organization to assist in connecting you with their colleagues whom lead a prospect organization.

BRINGING IT TO LIFE

◉ **Expect The Dots To Connect:** When you are in the people business, expect that people and relationships will connect. If not in the *short-term*, then absolutely in the *long-term*. Every new colleague or business partner represents a relationship that could shape you or your business today, several months later, or even several years down the road. Expect to have the opportunity to bring them value, and look for ways to offer something in the short-term, knowing that the relationship could blossom into the unexpected in the long-term. I recently attended a business dinner and was seated next to an individual I had never met. We hit it off immediately, and he shared that he leads new business strategy for a major national retailer. In less than three weeks both of our executive teams had met and mapped out a partnership strategy. We executed on that plan several months later. All of this simply because we both attended an executive connection event and happened to be seated together. *Do you expect the dots to connect? Do you walk into events with an open mind?*

◉ **In The Moment:** Expect that when you are not at *work events,* you are still representing your brand and your company's brand, and that you could possibly meet an individual who will propel your business or career. Continually strive to be open and intentionally listen to not only the names of the people whom you meet, but also the companies and businesses for which they work. It's always a great time to make a quality connection. *Are you perpetually in the moment and aware of whom you are meeting?*

◉ **Step Out:** If you are sitting at home, you will never expand your network. Get involved. Explore. Volunteer. Try something new. Get involved in industry leadership events. Engage in executive leadership organizations. You will never know the value of involvement until you experience it, and are able to gauge the value of investing your time versus the return in relationships developed. *What are you doing to fill your "involvement funnel" regularly? Are you cutting out the things that do not make sense from a content perspective, or represent environments where you cannot truly add value?*

BOTTOM LINE
Expected the unexpected.

CHAPTER 17

BIG IDEA!

CULTURE STARTS WITH THE LEADER

"Extraordinary leadership is inspiring trust while unleashing the right talent within aligned systems towards a clear and defined purpose. A leader must have extraordinary character so that those that share the vision and mission never question their inner confidence in the leader. Trust, confidence, and belief in a leader results in extraordinary accomplishments by ordinary people."
– Michael Faber, CEO, Viking Coca-Cola Bottling Company and First Choice Food & Beverage Solutions

There is a direct correlation between a leader's approach and the organization's culture. The leader sets the pace – the pulse of the organization's culture.

In thinking about culture, you as the leader must first recognize that *excellence* – the definition of extraordinary behavior expected in the business culture – must be very clearly defined by *you*. Every member of the organization has a different reference point for excellence, based on the environment in which they have been working. And that may not be consistent with *your* definition of excellence. For example, if a team member has been working in a Hilton Garden Inn, their reference point for customer excellence may be much different than that of someone who has spent their career working in a Conrad or Waldorf Astoria.

Second, the leader sets the pace and tempo of the culture. The leader defines the vision and related strategies to execute on that vision. The leader establishes the framework for communication routines and the operational cadence. The leader establishes the *fun* factor or lack thereof! The leader prioritizes people, product, portfolio, and process initiatives. The leader encourages specific behaviors, while not supporting others. The leader chooses to invest in knowing people; those who are raising the bar and those who could be doing better. Or the leader can choose to prioritize product, process, and portfolio over people. The leader listens, or else he/she is soon surrounded by a team that has nothing to say. The leader sets the pace.

Look at some of the very best company cultures and you will find that the vibe starts at the top with the leader. Very few organizational cultures operate opposite that of the leader. And the ones that attempt to do so, quickly fail.

Culture is something that evolves over time. The greatest moments of culture shift take place when a leadership change takes place. Extraordinary organizational cultures are destroyed in days and weeks when new leadership fails to take advantage of the organization's strengths, instead of driving change to eliminate its weaknesses. Top talent departs. Customers abandon formerly strong partnerships. Culture currents can make or break an organization. The leader that fails to recognize the power of positive culture is the leader that will be supported by the underperforming team.

BRINGING IT TO LIFE

◙ **Read The Currents:** As the leader, it is important to get a sense for the culture currents within the organization. You accomplish this by investing time with members of the team beyond your direct reports. Regularly take individuals to lunch, meet for coffee, and engage in check-in conversations. While many are *managing up*, focus on managing up, down, and sideways, as this is the only true way to build trust and know the people and the organization culture. Ask questions. Listen to responses and learn from them. Inevitably you will pick up nuggets – facts, figures, views, and opinions – that will help to shape your view of the organizational culture currents. *Do you understand what might be driving negative culture currents in your organization? Do you understand what is fueling the positive flow of energy within the organization?* The problems you don't know about are the problems you can't fix.

◙ **Conceptualize Your Desired Culture:** When taking on a new organizational role, one great culture exercise is to start by evaluating the current culture. Then define how you would ideally see your culture's future, and the impact you would like to see it have; both internally and externally. *What words frame up your culture vision?* Then focus on people and supporting processes that bring the elements of culture to the organization or team.

When others describe your organization's culture, what words would they use? Do these words match your desired culture state? Would they describe you as someone who sets the culture tone?

◉ **Talent Load:** It is important to identify those individuals who contribute to the makings of an extraordinary culture. Those that bring energy. Those that bring ideas. Those that enjoy challenging the process. Those that know how to balance fun with results. Not everyone contributes to a winning, growing, extraordinary organization culture. Some lead the negative naysayer parade. Others embrace office drama and gossip. Some just fail to act. You must make tough decisions about people to ensure that the culture is not destroyed by the minority. *Do you know who your culture killers are? Are you taking action to address them?*

◉ **Hire Up:** The loss of one team member provides an opportunity to seek out the next extraordinary up-and-comer. Use this opportunity to find the next person who will challenge the team and raise the bar. There is nothing more fun than watching a new, positive, high-octane performer join the organization, and then seeing the overall organization respond *positively*. By adding that one person to the organization, a team becomes a higher performing team, and the overall organization grows stronger as a result. *What will you do differently the next time you have an opportunity to add to your team?*

◙ **Invest In Culture-Building Activities:**
While people are the most important aspect of culture, there is no mistaking that company processes and procedures inherently *support* or *inhibit* culture. For example, a company culture filled with frequent town hall meetings, regular team meetings, leadership development and skill-building opportunities, frequent guest speakers, support services, and more, make it possible for extraordinary people to achieve more than extraordinary business results. *How often is culture a conversation between you and HR? What activities are in place to drive employee engagement?*

BOTTOM LINE
Extraordinary culture attracts extraordinary talent.

EXCEPTIONAL. REMARKABLE.
PHENOMENAL. UNUSUAL.
IMPACTFUL. INCOMPARABLE.
WONDERFUL. NOTABLE. MARVELOUS.
LIMITLESS. FANTASTIC. CURIOUS.
OUTSTANDING. DIFFERENTIATED.
OVER-THE-TOP. UNCOMMON.
SINGULAR. SURPRISING. SPECIAL.
ASTONISHING. RARE. UNIQUE.
UNPRECEDENTED. AMAZING. VIVID.
STRONG. MEMORABLE. INCREDIBLE.
AN ANOMALY.

**A DECISION. A CHOICE.
THAT'S EXTRAORDINARY.**

CHAPTER 18

BIG IDEA!
WASHEY-WASHEY, HAPPY-HAPPY

"Extraordinary leadership is surrounding yourself with
strong, positive, smart people, and listening to them. Extraordinary
leadership is confidently following your instincts, while maintaining
a sense of humility. Extraordinary leadership is being true to
yourself and those around you at all times."

– Cathy Marder, Associate Publisher, RIS News

"Give me an hour on a ship and I can tell you the mood or vibe of the ship's crew," said Chief Engineer Rolf of Norwegian Cruise Lines.

The Norwegian *Pearl* cruise ship was completed on November 28, 2006, in the Meyer Werft Shipyard in Papenburg, Germany, after two years of construction at a cost of $528 million. A flagship of Norwegian Cruise Lines, she carries 1,100+ crew and serves between 2,000-3,000 guests weekly on voyages spanning the globe.

These numbers, however, are not what caught my attention on a recent Caribbean cruise on the *Pearl*. What I experienced and observed throughout seven days and six nights on the ship was the overwhelmingly positive attitude and overall disposition of every single staff member I interacted with on-board the ship. Each person went out of his or her way to say "hello," to offer assistance, to check in on our on-board experience, and to engage us in conversation. They picked up on small nuances of our family, such as our preferences at dinner and in the cabin. They mixed fun activities, events, excursions, and parties with extraordinary customer service.

Most of the staff serves in multiple guest service roles 24/7 on-board the ship. But I was curious to understand the *secret sauce* that fueled such an amazing environment. And so, I asked.

During a "Learn How to Run a Cruise Ship" session on the final day of the trip, Captain Rune, Chief Engineer Rolf, Hotel Director Tony, and Cruise Director Julie discussed leadership on a cruise ship. They outlined a number of key elements as to what it takes to create and sustain an extraordinary staff organization on board. Not surprisingly, it starts at the top with having the right leadership team.

BRINGING IT TO LIFE

◉ **It Starts With The Senior Leadership Team:** For a few moments, we were out of *vacation vocabulary* and into *business speak* as the leaders of the ship's team immediately embraced my atypical question. "What drives extraordinary guest experience on-board the boat?" Each chose to answer my question, and the first common theme was that the environment, the approach to guest service, and the overall organizational culture starts with the *leaders*. As the leaders lead, the employees follow or move on. In the case of the *Pearl,* the best choose to stay and develop their careers in that positive environment. At the same time, the leadership reinforced the value of engaging the team up and down the organizational structure and highlighted that any weak links in the guest service chain result in a poor guest experience on board.

◉ **Fun, Fun, Fun:** Fun is not limited to the guests. A staff member is assigned to organizing events, activities, and outings for the staff. Regular social events are planned on board, and when in port, the staff often engages with other NCL crews in competitive games and activities. Furthermore, each week the staff members are offered the opportunity to formally showcase their talents on the cruise ship's main stage for the guests. A talent show, of sorts, which give the staff an opportunity to demonstrate their unique artistic talents and skills. Happy employees translate into happy guests and extraordinary experiences.

◉ **Export Talent:** Like major organizations, exporting talent is a priority with NCL. It's a way to share positive principles and guest service best practices with other parts of the organization. The leadership team shared the importance of developing and retaining top talent on the ship.

Staff members also discussed the value of moving between ships and the corporate office to further their career.

◉ **"Wash It Out Clean":** When Chief Engineer Rolf made his opening statement, I asked about his experience on other ships. He stated, "The only way to change the culture of the shipboard crew is to completely wash it out. Wash it out clean. I can read whether or not a ship is a *happy* ship very quickly." He followed with observations on the importance of bringing on the right team members that meet and elevate the team: not much different than what we subscribe to in the business world. He clearly stated the importance of *shipping out* the bad apples quickly – perhaps a lesson that more companies could learn and apply. Guests rely on the crew for fun, as they have paid for extraordinary experiences. Guests rely on crew for safety and their lives are literally in the hands of those who know emergency procedures. In the cruise business, there really is no room for a weak link on the team.

◉ **P.S.:** In case you were wondering about the "Washey-Washey, Happy-Happy, Smiley-Smiley, All the Time!" phrase that names this chapter, here's the story: The crew of the *Pearl* wrote their *own* song to make a monotonous and potentially annoying activity fun. At all times, a set group of crew members is responsible for spraying the hands of each guest with disinfectant as they enter the main dining room. They call this "Washey-Washey." They sing the song throughout the day as you enter the restaurant, simply called, "Washey-Washey, Smiley-Smiley, Happy-Happy, All the Time." Creative. Fun. By the end of the week, guests and crew alike could be seen repeating this phrase and singing this song as they entered the dining room. This is a great lesson in making something that is so necessary and simple, and frankly mundane, turn into something fun and memorable!

BOTTOM LINE

Extraordinary experiences
are rooted in happy employees.

EXCEPTIONAL. REMARKABLE.
PHENOMENAL. UNUSUAL.
IMPACTFUL. INCOMPARABLE.
WONDERFUL. NOTABLE. MARVELOUS.
LIMITLESS. FANTASTIC. CURIOUS.
OUTSTANDING. DIFFERENTIATED.
OVER-THE-TOP. UNCOMMON.
SINGULAR. SURPRISING. SPECIAL.
ASTONISHING. RARE. UNIQUE.
UNPRECEDENTED. AMAZING. VIVID.
STRONG. MEMORABLE. INCREDIBLE.
AN ANOMALY.

**A DECISION. A CHOICE.
THAT'S EXTRAORDINARY.**

CHAPTER 19

BIG IDEA!
VISION CLARIFIES DESTINATION

"Extraordinary leadership is sacrificial. It leads with the motivation
to serve, desiring only what is best for those who follow."
— Justin Grunewald, Pastor, Buckhead Church

No vision, no direction. I am a firm believer that no organization can exist successfully without a well-defined vision. The vision is a destination. It is a state that sometimes stretches the team – perhaps out of their comfort zone – yet is aspirational. As the leader, it is your responsibility to set a clear, easy-to-understand vision for the team or organization. It must be one that is easy-to-understand, repeat, and communicate; not only within the organization, but also with customers and supporting constituents. The vision essentially provides a solution to problems or challenges that already exist; or supports the overall organizational vision that has been established.

I refine and reset the vision statement for our team each year. As the leader, I want to provide clarity and focus for the team. We have a collaboration session to define the strategies, activities, and metrics that enable pursuit of the vision. We all own the end product which is a one page vision summary. We regularly review, communicate, and share our vision with others in the organization. There should be no confusion, because we have defined it simply. It is portable and simple. An organization without a vision is like a rudderless ship with no destination. A vision gives team members something to rally around and work toward; to be a part of; to own.

As the leader, you must regularly *vision-cast* and find communication outlets to reinforce the vision. This could also include introducing new strategic ideas for collaboration and a central focus-for-the-month to provide a better framework for the team to work toward achieving the vision. Plans and strategies can change along the path, but the vision always stays the same. And you, as the leader, are commissioned to own, lead, reinforce, and apply the vision. Your vision must be a solution to a problem being faced by your organization, by your customers, or by your business partners. *How much time do you annually allocate to set, refine, and communicate your vision?*

BRINGING IT TO LIFE

◉ **Define It:** Many will have ideas and input on what the organizational vision should be. My recommendation is that you establish the top-line vision statement, explain and validate it with the leadership team, then make tweaks as necessary. Finally, involve the leadership team in defining the strategies and tactics that the organization will employ in pursuit of the vision.

◉ **Make It Portable:** Many organizations maintain a mission statement that supports the overall vision. Most are way too long and not easy to remember, repeat, or share. They lose their value in the overall context of organization strategy. Keep it simple. Keep it focused. Keep it portable. Leverage it and repeat it as part of your regular communication routine.

◉ **Define The Bottom Line:** Once the vision, strategies, tactics, and organizational hand-offs are established, try defining a bottom line that sums up *what it's all about*. Or complete this sentence: "At the end of the day, we are all about XYZ."

BOTTOM LINE

Vision-casting must be part of the leader's routine.

EXCEPTIONAL. REMARKABLE.
PHENOMENAL. UNUSUAL.
IMPACTFUL. INCOMPARABLE.
WONDERFUL. NOTABLE. MARVELOUS.
LIMITLESS. FANTASTIC. CURIOUS.
OUTSTANDING. DIFFERENTIATED.
OVER-THE-TOP. UNCOMMON.
SINGULAR. SURPRISING. SPECIAL.
ASTONISHING. RARE. UNIQUE.
UNPRECEDENTED. AMAZING. VIVID.
STRONG. MEMORABLE. INCREDIBLE.
AN ANOMALY.

A DECISION. A CHOICE.
THAT'S EXTRAORDINARY.

CHAPTER 20

BIG IDEA!
NO TRUST, NO TEAM

"Extraordinary leadership is a gift. It's a gift to others in an
organization as it enables them to run efficiently and effectively.
This gift helps associates understand what is expected of them and
encourages them to achieve consistently positive results. Extraordinary
leaders serve as an example for others to follow and encourage
associates to build their own leadership skills. Extraordinary leadership is
a characteristic that is often innate, but can be improved upon over time
by focusing on personal development. It is a characteristic that is regularly
shaped by events that challenge us as individuals."

– Jim Marvel, Region Vice President, Coca-Cola Refreshments

Without trust, there is no team. Trust is founded on communication, and without a solid communication framework, there is no trust. As a leader, you will differentiate yourself from others by establishing communication routines as a fundamental core competence of your organization.

Share the facts. Share the details. Too many leaders operate with a *knowledge is power* mentality and solely share with others on a *need-to-know* basis. The best leaders I have worked with are those who share openly. They make you feel as if you truly are a trusted part of the team, and the resulting loyalty drives incredible results. Knowledge and information are powerful, and when used properly, drive intense, positive engagement with the organization.

Cautious leaders worry about how their messages may be misconstrued or misunderstood and, consequently, fail to communicate in an authentic manner. This only serves to increase the likelihood that the message is misconstrued. Most people want to know the facts and desire a culture of trust – for better or worse. Leaders fail when they disregard the importance of trust, or fear the communication effort involved in extending trust. Trust is ultimately defined by the maturity and actions of the organization leader.

You must *extend* trust to *receive* trust in return. More importantly, trust is something that takes time to build. Ultimately, it can be destroyed in seconds. Team trust fuels momentum. And lack of team trust often leads to a lack of progress. Without trust, a leader will only hear the *positive* side of situations. People will fear sharing anything negative because they fear the response.

In my management consulting days, I worked on a team that had a leader who would literally yell at individuals for dropping the ball on a task, no matter how small. The result was that trust was quickly lost within the team. Communication up and down the organization completely stopped, and the team failed to produce the results we were capable of producing. Trust, the foundational element of success of any team, was not in place.

In another instance, I was a part of a team that

appeared to lack trust among its organization's members for no better reason than a simple lack of communication between the leader and the team members. While not intentional, facts and figures were known by some but not by others. People wondered why some people had information and others didn't. Questions arose. Doubts lingered. Because of communication gaps (unintended inconsistencies) on the team, trust started to erode.

The remarkable and most interesting element of the situation was that the leader recognized that trust among the team members was lacking, so he proactively took actions to address it. He first made trust a foundational element of every team meeting. He outlined what trust meant to him and how it would be defined within our team. He repeated it regularly and engaged each of us to identify ways in which we could invest in the *trust quotient* within our own teams. Second, he formally held each of us accountable for building trust; not only with others on the leadership team, but also with others in our organization. Over the course of several months the team atmosphere changed dramatically. Members were open and honest, with both positive and constructive feedback. We were much more collaborative. Projects moved faster. Decisions were made quickly. The *fun* factor and camaraderie increased exponentially across the organization.

Simply recognizing that the of lack of trust existed, then being dedicated to defining trust and making it a core value for our team, drove significant positive impact within our work environment. Furthermore, encouraging communication on the topic and publicly recognizing the wins that resulted was a true testament to his leadership.

BRINGING IT TO LIFE

◉ **Live It Out:** Find a way to define the importance of trust for your team or organization. Consider using Stephen Covey's book *The Speed of Trust*[3] as a *thought starter* to discuss the importance of trust. Incorporate exercises on trust into team meetings. Proactively discuss trust gaps in your organization. High trust yields a *trust dividend* evidenced by increased performance. Low trust yields a *trust tax* that results in poor overall performance. *Are you paying dividends or raising taxes?*

◉ **Communicate It:** If trust is important, it must be part of the leadership communication cadence of the organization. As the leader, trust must be part of the strategy plan that enables the vision. This should be part of regular communications as an element that takes the team to extraordinary. *How do you reinforce the importance of trust? How do you recognize the value of trust and ensure associated actions are repeated?*

◉ **Model It:** When you extend trust to others, they will extend trust to you. They will share information, views, opinions, ideas, and even performance feedback with you; but only if you are open to receiving it through a trust-based relationship. *Are you open to trusting others? Actions speak.*

◉ **Be Consistent:** Nothing is more frustrating than a leader whose communication methods and processes are always changing. Staying consistent helps the organization and related teams know what to expect and when to expect it.

BOTTOM LINE
Trust makes or breaks a leader ... and a team.

EXCEPTIONAL. REMARKABLE.
PHENOMENAL. UNUSUAL.
IMPACTFUL. INCOMPARABLE.
WONDERFUL. NOTABLE. MARVELOUS.
LIMITLESS. FANTASTIC. CURIOUS.
OUTSTANDING. DIFFERENTIATED.
OVER-THE-TOP. UNCOMMON.
SINGULAR. SURPRISING. SPECIAL.
ASTONISHING. RARE. UNIQUE.
UNPRECEDENTED. AMAZING. VIVID.
STRONG. MEMORABLE. INCREDIBLE.
AN ANOMALY.

**A DECISION. A CHOICE.
THAT'S EXTRAORDINARY.**

CHAPTER 21

BIG IDEA!
COACHING AND LISTENING

"Extraordinary leadership has always been about being honest, being convicted about your purpose, and making sure you do not get distracted by outside influences. Above all, it must be Christian-based, so as not to crumble during the course of action."

– Chan Gailey, Head Football Coach, National Football League

Good leaders make it a point to coach others. We've covered that. But great leaders accept coaching *from* others, including their direct reports. They also take time to *listen*. Leaders who fail to listen will very quickly be surrounded by a team of individuals who have nothing to say, who provide no input, who shut down, and who choose to leave.

Effective listening is core to being an effective coach. *Are you the type of leader who is passionate about helping others to develop in their personal and professional endeavors? When coaching and mentoring others, do you encourage them to define their brand, to understand their passion points, and to recognize areas where they may need to invest to shore up knowledge, skills, or experience gaps?* When they are able to do this, and as they pursue new career opportunities, they inevitably bring more than a resume to the interview table. They are able to bring knowledge of whom they are – from the inside-out – and clearly communicate their leadership style, what motivates them, what they are passionate about, and what they count as strengths and development needs.

There is a timing element to effective feedback and coaching. As a leader, it is imperative to provide coaching *immediately* when an action is taken. The feedback is timely, and allows the individual to internalize it as it relates to the recent action. Some individuals hold onto individual feedback then deliver it in a one-to-one meeting at a *later* date. This dilutes its effectiveness and can result in distrust between the employee and manager. When providing coaching or feedback, it is imperative to not only identify and acknowledge the improvement opportunity, but also to provide insight into what can be done to resolve it.

Have you ever been in a meeting where the leader dominates the discussion? You attempt to share your great idea or opinion and the leader talks over you. The leader fails to acknowledge your idea or how it could be utilized. In fact, the leader's way is the only way. *Have you ever worked for a leader that needs feedback? Needs someone to coach them on how to be a better presenter? Needs someone to share with them an observed communication quirk or nuance? Needs someone to inform them of key culture currents at play outside of the leader's purview?* If the leader does not ask, you cannot offer. The leader must seek to listen, extend trust, and have a sincere desire to become better.

There appears to be two challenges here, but in fact the one central issue is the lack of the leader's intentional efforts to listen and engage. Some leaders are centrally focused on managing upward and fail to listen to the needs of their own team. Other leaders are so centrally focused on one business idea, product, or solution that they lose focus of the proverbial forest. Even leaders get hung up in managing their own career amidst the fog of internal politics. They may even relegate the team or organization to second priority.

While it is important to provide perspectives to others, it is equally important to actively listen to others in order to understand how you personally can improve. In one of my professional roles, I had the opportunity to build a new team. As we began performing as a team, I introduced an activity that I called a "Personal SWOT (Strengths-Weaknesses-Opportunities-Threats)." Step one was providing a one-page, four-box model to each team member. I asked them to list their *strengths* (individual characteristics that give them an advantage), their *weaknesses* (individual characteristics that place them at a disadvantage), their *opportunities* (where they could improve their performance), and their *threats* (elements that could trouble them or put their success in the role at risk). Step two was asking them to complete a similar page for *every other* team member, including me. We proceeded to share our observations, feedback, and recommendations to each member of the team verbally. It was an extraordinary exercise. There was such a raw level of trust and accountability present in our discussions. The results went well beyond feedback and recommendations, and served to establish a bond on our team that could not be artificially manufactured.

As the leader, much can be learned when you listen, crave feedback, and desire to raise the game of your team members. Knowledge develops through effective listening.

BRINGING IT TO LIFE

◉ **Leadership Assimilation:** *As a new leader, have you engaged in a formal process called Leadership Assimilation (a formal program to quickly introduce and launch a new leader with a new team)?* This is a great way for you to establish communication and trust with a team, and gain fast first-impression feedback that can set the stage for an extraordinary team environment. *As an experienced leader, have you had a formal 360 review completed?* This allows for a semi-anonymous review of your performance by peers, colleagues, and team members, and highlights actionable development opportunities. Extraordinary leaders grasp the improvement opportunities with the same, if not greater, vigor as the positives in developing out a personal development and team engagement plan.

◉ **Be Timely:** Get over any fears or concerns about having timely crucial conversations with your peers and team members. View your ability to provide coaching and feedback to others as a gift that will help the individual to grow, develop, and succeed. Be timely in providing feedback versus waiting for a future date to provide the coaching. *When was the last time you provided timely feedback? Is there a reason why you are waiting to give someone feedback?*

◉ **Give Permissions:** If you do not ask for feedback and coaching from others, especially peers and direct or indirect reports, then don't expect to receive it. Oftentimes, people feel as if they must have your permission to give you feedback. Leaders who do not open themselves up to receiving feedback and coaching will never receive it; especially from direct reports who fear that feedback could be misconstrued and become a career-limiting move. How you respond to feedback will directly correlate to whether or not you continue to receive feedback in the future. Consider your response carefully.

◉ **Model It:** When I initiated the "Personal SWOT" activity, the team was understandably anxious. The first thing I did was to be overtly honest and constructive in evaluating a member of our team, then I asked for the same in return. Ice broken. What followed was one of the most powerful experiences and conversations I have ever been a part of in leading a team. *Are you modeling both giving and receiving feedback?*

BOTTOM LINE

Be timely. Be specific. Listen.

CHAPTER 22

BIG IDEA!
ATTITUDE AND ENCOURAGEMENT

"Extraordinary leadership is putting yourself in the shoes
of the people you lead. It means learning what it's like to do their
job and lending a hand whenever possible. This builds solidarity,
as people feel that you're 'for them.' It shows them that you genuinely
understand their successes and struggles."
– Mike Tiemann, UpStreet Production Director, Buckhead Church

---

Certain people thrive in environments where they have the opportunity to work with others who bring a positive, make-things-happen attitude and energy. Unfortunately, it is often the people who fail to bring that internal energy who are the first ones to roll their eyes at individuals who naturally bring positive energy to meetings, working sessions, and discussions. High energy is sometimes dismissed as silly, unprofessional, immature, overdone, too optimistic, or not realistic.

High energy, when demonstrated properly, is absolutely a brand asset. The key is to determine the best way to leverage your natural positive energy and understand how you leverage the people on your team who bring this attribute to the table. A leader is able to synthesize high-octane performers who bring different levels of energy, skill, and ability to the organization.

One leader I know had a team member, amidst a team of rock star performers, who brought a level of natural energy that far exceeded that of others. He was often criticized as lacking professional maturity, but the reality was that he had a unique level of energy and a relationship-oriented ability to connect with people in a way that many others do not naturally bring to the table. It's important to regularly coach individuals like this to ensure that their energy is not lost or suppressed due to misguided feedback. I have seen a number of individuals over time who have become negative, quiet, or simply disconnected as they succumbed to the constant drumbeat of negativity, criticism, or "get back in your box" coaching.

As a leader of a team or organization, encouragement and a positive attitude are critical leadership techniques for building effective teams. *Have you ever worked for a boss, who gives you very little feedback on your performance; who rarely shared what you are doing well; or what you need to improve? Or have you ever worked for a boss who regularly provided feedback, but always of the negative variety?*

Naturally, individuals appreciate being appreciated. Most people have enough challenging situations in life that where they spend the majority of their life each week should be positive, meaningful, and constructive. As much as constructive criticism is important, ongoing and regular recognition of efforts, results, and differentiated performance is also important. This keeps the team motivated through the ups and downs of the corporate or start-up environment.

As the leader, actions and behaviors are the by-product of attitude. If you start the day with a negative attitude; frustrated at the world and unhappy with life, your team will feel it, see it, and experience it. Start the day with a positive attitude. Look for ways to solve problems, generate new energy, and achieve small accomplishments on the way to the big win. Your team will feel it, and over time, engage you in it.

Check your attitude daily to ensure you are staying on the right side of the dial. Avoid spending time with colleagues who are complaining or criticizing. Disconnect from situations that could lead you down a path to the left side of the attitude dial. Bring passion. Bring energy. Bring engagement. Dial it up.

BRINGING IT TO LIFE

◉ **Attitude Check:** Set aside time on a regular basis to review what has gone well, what lessons you have learned from successes and accomplishments, and what mistakes you have made – both personally and professionally. This is valuable time to assess what personal development opportunities you must address. *Are you operating with a positive attitude? Or has your negativity been apparent to others?*

◉ **Positive Attitude Changes Everything (PACE):** I learned the PACE concept as a high school student at a YMCA camp in the North Carolina Mountains. This was the first time I was exposed to feedback, perception, and the idea that a positive attitude can truly change everything: every problem, every relationship, and every challenging situation. When I, the leader, demonstrate and operate with a positive attitude, it absolutely rubs off on the team, customers, and partners with whom I work. It takes much more energy to be negative, and the effects are often long-lasting and consequential. When a team member does great work, I recognize them for it publicly. When they make mistakes, we discuss what we learned from it and move on privately. We are a team.

◉ **Avoid "Those" People:** Draw a large T on a sheet of paper. On one side write a + and on the other, a –. Add the names of your friends, family, and business colleagues to the positive or the negative side of the page, depending on whether this person buoys you up or weighs you down. This simple exercise will help you identify relationships that you should flag as potentially holding you back, weighing you down, or disallowing you from achieving the extraordinary. It will also highlight those relationships that help you move forward in life by helping you feel appreciated, loved, and needed. Leaders surround themselves with others that can help them accomplish the extraordinary.

◉ **What Is Rewarded Is Repeated:** Rewarded or encouraged behavior is repeated behavior. This is a simple concept that many of us have learned from having pets. In the workplace, it is especially true with talent management structures and performance review processes. Actions, behaviors, and decisions that are rewarded are repeated. Good behavior, wise decisions, and people-oriented actions are rewarded and recognized. This leads to their recurrence in the workplace. This is a crucial concept that many *drivers* or leaders that lack people skills often overlook – one difference between ordinary versus extraordinary leadership. We need to celebrate our wins and recognize those that go above and beyond. And remember that *when you recognize everyone, you recognize no one.*

◉ **Clarify The Win:** In this case, what's first is last. It all starts with clarifying the win (the ideal future state). In most businesses, performance objectives, talent profiles, and career objectives are established for each individual. Identify the objectives, agree to review progress regularly, and hold each other accountable for completing the play. In each case, start by clarifying the win. *What are you doing so that these wins are quantitatively and qualitatively measureable? Are you reviewing these throughout the year? Can you articulate what the win looks like?*

BOTTOM LINE

There is a direct correlation
between attitude and results.

EXCEPTIONAL. REMARKABLE.
PHENOMENAL. UNUSUAL.
IMPACTFUL. INCOMPARABLE.
WONDERFUL. NOTABLE. MARVELOUS.
LIMITLESS. FANTASTIC. CURIOUS.
OUTSTANDING. DIFFERENTIATED.
OVER-THE-TOP. UNCOMMON.
SINGULAR. SURPRISING. SPECIAL.
ASTONISHING. RARE. UNIQUE.
UNPRECEDENTED. AMAZING. VIVID.
STRONG. MEMORABLE. INCREDIBLE.
AN ANOMALY.

A DECISION. A CHOICE.
THAT'S EXTRAORDINARY.

CHAPTER 23

BIG IDEA!
LIFE RESETS ARE BRAND ASSETS

"Extraordinary leadership stands out! It is having extraordinary character, a strong moral compass, the ability to create passion in others, to drive commitment, to harness and exploit positive energy. It's having a strong will, fortitude, tenacity, integrity. It is not conceited. It is a passion for learning. Extraordinary leadership embraces change. It exudes an enthusiasm and a confidence that makes others want to follow."
— Monique Honaman, Partner, ISHR Group

Life *resets* are a guarantee. They are not optional. What's *not* guaranteed is how you handle these resets. *What do you learn from them? How do you let them affect you? How do you move forward with them as part of your life story?* The only way to learn from experiences is to take time to reflect upon them.

Starting over is never easy. Sometimes it's necessary, and it's not always by choice. All of us, at some point in our lives, are forced to make difficult decisions that involve a reset or a restart. This is essentially the demolition of some existing practice and the start of something new. For some, it could be the death of a loved one. For others, it might be the illness of a significant other, a divorce, or a lost job.

Consider divorce. Every situation is different. And while some share commonalities in what ultimately led to a failed marriage, they occur for reasons that are often unexplainable to those not in the situation. The questions are these: *How do the involved individuals handle life after divorce? What did they learn? What can they apply to the next relationship?*

Resets can also involve illness and the loss of a loved one. My godmother had just completed a memorable trip, hiking through the Swiss Alps. On her flight home she experienced a severe stomach ache and thought she may have pulled a muscle. She decided to see her doctor to get medication. Instead of simply prescribing pain medication, the doctor ran tests and diagnosed her with pancreatic cancer. She had only weeks to live. Two months later, she passed away. *What do you do with that? How does that even make sense?*

Over the past year I have spoken with several career transition groups. Given our economic downturn, so many people have lost their jobs and are struggling to reset or reboot their careers. Many of these individuals had never planned for this type of reset. They were looking for the positive in a situation that, at times, appeared to have no light at the end of the tunnel. Individuals who proactively approached the transition period tended to find their next opportunity quickly. Individuals who invested in relationships and helped others tended to find their next opportunity quickly. Individuals who recognized that they couldn't control what happened to them, but rather how they chose to react to it, tended to find their next opportunity quickly.

Those who were looking for an easy out or quick fix, who dwelled on the negative, who were selfish in their job search, were the ones who were panicking because they didn't seem to be finding their next opportunity.

Life resets will happen. While you can't control the ins and outs of life resets, you can approach them in a way that results in learning from each one. Life plans will change. And yet your vision for your life, your hopes, and your dreams should remain the same. You can't control what happens to you. But you can control how you respond to it.

BRINGING IT TO LIFE

- ◉ **What You Can Control:** During any life reset, start by asking: *What can I control? What is beyond my control?* There are absolutely things you cannot control, and in working through a challenging situation, you must find short-term wins. The biggest challenge for any of us working through a life reset is to avoid letting the uncontrollable things weigh us down and keep us from moving forward.

- ◉ **Navigate Change:** When going through any major change, you may face any number of emotions as you roll through denial, fear, anxiety, confusion, acceptance, new energy, and even positive feelings. The timing of the cycle is not predictable, but every reset has its peaks and valleys. The optimist must find a way to find those peaks and hold tight through the valleys. The positive moments are fuel to long-term recovery.

◉ **Vision . . . And Plans:** We all have visions for our life. Short-term visions of what our day will look like tomorrow. Medium-term visions of finally getting into shape, achieving the next level at work, or going on a dream vacation. Long-term visions of seeing a business grow, finding love, or seeing the kids graduate from college. Visions are powerful, fun, and provide life's momentum. The challenge comes when plans change; especially when you aren't expecting them. *How do you respond? Are you flexible and adaptable? Do you look for alternative routes and are you open to new ideas?* Remember this: while your plans in life will change, and your path to achieving your vision will change, your vision remains constant.

BOTTOM LINE
Reset. Reboot. Restart.

CHAPTER 24

BIG IDEA!
WIN WHEN YOU LOSE

"Extraordinary leadership is getting as close as possible to aligning your God-given abilities with your own deeply understood sense of purpose; and then acting on it."

– Albert Guffanti, Group Publisher, Edgell Communications

I hate losing. I was eight days into my new role when I was handed a half-baked deal with a small niche customer with less than a week to go before a final decision would be made on the partnership. We brought price to the table but the the competitor brought a better price. Not good.

This was definitely one of those fly-by-the-seat-of-your-pants moments. I really did not know enough about our assets or our processes, or even about how to pull in the added-value components of our business to the deal table. Our competitor won by offering additional dollars. This was a deal that we could have easily won with the right people, process, focus, and solutions that addressed the customer's objectives, goals, and challenges. The customer even told us that they wanted us to win, but defaulted to the competitor based on price when we failed to deliver the value solution.

We lost … and I hated it. This was a valuable lesson in selling, as the partnership needed to be centered on more than price. It needed to be a *total partner program*. It needed to address the customer's core business challenges. It needed to center on more than product and service cost. It needed to include solutions to challenges the customer was facing with its consumer. It needed to include a strategy for addressing a multi-channel consumer. It needed to include joint marketing and global growth objectives. And, of course, it needed to be a partnership centered on mutual financial gains.

We celebrate wins. We document wins. We outline best practices that result in wins. And yet the lessons in loss are just as important. Never fail to *analyze* and *evaluate* why you fail to win. It is just as important as the analysis of drivers that drove success.

BRINGING IT TO LIFE

- ◉ **Engage Strategically:** Strategic partnerships are built with strategic decision-makers; not buyers and procurement managers. You have to start top-down or be prepared to be stuck in a price battle that drives profit-less business relationships. *Are you engaging at the right level?*

- ◉ **Debrief:** Whether there is a meeting, working session, presentation, or any other type of customer collaboration, there is immense value in a transparent debrief session. Nobody is perfect and every situation – win or lose – is a learning opportunity for the future. This should include personal as well as program or organizational lessons learned. It is the responsibility of the leader to organize and lead the debrief. Be aware that the tendency is to avoid the after-action discussion if the deal has been lost (nobody wants to dwell on bad news). *Do you take time to complete the lessons learned discussion before racing to the next opportunity? How quickly do you pull it together and what structure do you use to drive the discussion and evaluation?*

◉ **Stay In Touch:** The best losers become the future winners. In the example above, our primary business stakeholder was promoted several months after the decision was made regarding our potential partnership. I immediately wrote her a congratulatory note. She replied with surprise and appreciation. She even mentioned that our competition would never even recognize something so small which, in reality, was a huge deal to her. Small things add up! *Are you staying in touch?*

BOTTOM LINE
Success is when preparation meets opportunity.

EXCEPTIONAL. REMARKABLE.
PHENOMENAL. UNUSUAL.
IMPACTFUL. INCOMPARABLE.
WONDERFUL. NOTABLE. MARVELOUS.
LIMITLESS. FANTASTIC. CURIOUS.
OUTSTANDING. DIFFERENTIATED.
OVER-THE-TOP. UNCOMMON.
SINGULAR. SURPRISING. SPECIAL.
ASTONISHING. RARE. UNIQUE.
UNPRECEDENTED. AMAZING. VIVID.
STRONG. MEMORABLE. INCREDIBLE.
AN ANOMALY.

A DECISION. A CHOICE.
THAT'S EXTRAORDINARY.

CHAPTER 25

BIG IDEA!
THE LEADERSHIP PIPELINE

"Extraordinary leadership is a way of being – not a way of commanding.
Humble – knowing we are better together. Other focused – finding that the
greatest calling of leadership is to help others succeed."

– S. Max Brown, Vice President, Organizational Learning, Rideau

---

Over the past three years, several of the business and philanthropic organizations in which I participate have gone through a strategic leadership change. Each has experienced a change at the very top of the organization.

Several of these organizations have experienced positive momentum after a leadership change. They are seeing new growth, increased engagement, and measurable financial results. They have moved beyond where they were, prior to the organizational change. They are creating new value, experiences, and interactions that benefit their constituents.

On the opposite end of the spectrum, two of the organizations have become stagnant at best. They are barely moving forward. Their constituents see it and recognize it.

The behaviors, actions, and qualities of the new

leader – be it a CEO, President, Chairman, General Manager, Headmaster, Principal, or Board Chair – are absolutely critical indicators of the future direction of the organization. The leaders that make a positive impact bring new energy and new ideas. They are engaged, active, interested, and intelligent. They are looking to add value, remove dead weight, and move the organization into places previously untraveled. Yet they are also careful to not let go of the critical qualities that propelled the organization to where it is today. They have the vision and the people skills to engage a team powered to move the organization beyond what was done in the past towards an all-new future.

Those failing are not charismatic. These leaders do not regularly engage with employees and outside customers/constituents, and have dropped many of the programs and initiatives that were part of the fabric of the organization. These leaders failed to survey the landscape. They failed to see what truly was working in the organization.

The reality is that the direction sailed by a ship can be influenced by wind and seas, but only directed and steered by the captain. Organization leadership is an unbelievably challenging task. The key to success is to cultivate a pipeline of backfill candidates for the top leadership roles, engage in development activities for those individuals, and make changes quickly if the leader is not working out.

BRINGING IT TO LIFE

◉ **Pipeline:** An organization without a pipeline of strong backfill candidates is one that is set up for failure with the loss of even *one* key member of the team. It is imperative that the organization have a structured, well thought-out, and reviewed/approved plan for the leadership talent pipeline. *Do you have a succession plan in place for your top leadership roles? How frequently is it reviewed and updated?*

◉ **Evaluation:** The leader is not only accountable to the shareholders, but also to customers, members, guests, employees, partners, and suppliers. Evaluation must absolutely be a part of any organization culture. Of course, evaluation begins by setting expectations and understanding critical success metrics, before evaluating both quantitative and qualitative aspects of the leader's performance. For example, the leader may achieve budget objectives and deliver positive overall financial objectives, but may not be engaging with customers in a way that ensures long-term success of the organization.

◉ **Energy:** I am a strong believer that energy and enthusiasm are two characteristics of successful leadership. *Are you bringing energy and enthusiasm to your organization and/or team? Are you viewed as a high-octane leader?*

BOTTOM LINE

Energy + Enthusiasm + Engagement =
Extraordinary.

CHAPTER 26

BIG IDEA!
ACTIONS HAVE CONSEQUENCES

"Extraordinary leadership is defined by leaders who lead by example. Those who are in leadership positions must keep in mind that team members will always model something or someone. Extraordinary leadership is recognizing this and considering the impact of decisions before they are made, as someone is always watching."

– Tony Marino, Founder, Trinity Web Works

My sister was at a Blackjack table in Las Vegas during a recent business trip. She was talking with others at the table who were attending the same technology conference and she mentioned the company for which she *formerly* worked. An SVP of Merchandising from a major specialty retailer at the table stated, "I will never give them my business again. Their sales rep outright lied to us about point-of-sale technology five years ago and we have not forgotten that. We will never meet with them again."

What I found compelling about this interaction was the fact that one error in judgment by a technology sales rep resulted in the loss of a major prospective customer's business. Furthermore, that experience was discussed and ultimately damaged the brand of that company. The retailer decided not to buy from them for several years. Decisions have intended and unintended consequences.

Last year I was sitting in the bleachers at a football game played by ten-year-olds. Suddenly, in the middle of the game, one of the assistant coaches objected to a call and ran onto the field to dispute the call. The referee immediately threw the coach out of the game. And then it happened. The assistant coach, in front of two teams of young boys and a stadium full of parents and siblings, unleashed an expletive-filled tirade that, to this day, ranks as one of the poorest demonstrations of leadership I have witnessed in youth athletics. He pulled his son out of the game, slammed the gate on his way off of the field, and proceeded to continue yelling and screaming while walking through the bleachers and sidelines as everyone watched in stark silence. A week later I attended a prayer breakfast. The guest speaker was introduced. Yep, you guessed it. It was none other than the coach. Ironically, he spoke on the value of patience, humility, and decision-making. Decisions have intended and unintended consequences.

Two weeks later I was in Dallas for a retail event. After the event, I met several colleagues to debrief at the hotel restaurant. A major computer hardware company was meeting at the same hotel and many of its attendees were also in the restaurant. Without getting into specifics, I will just say that the words and actions of this company's team were obnoxious, and represented more than just "fun on the road." Our impression of their company was very negative. And this was a company that everyone reading this book would recognize. When you wear the logo of a business, you represent the business. Your actions affect the value of that company's brand.

If you have ever traveled through the Sao Paulo airport in Brazil, you know that it is not the prime example of efficiency. Due to traffic, it can take hours to get to the airport. Once there, you can spend additional hours worming your way through security, check-in, and customs. One thing I love about travel is that I often witness amusing events! I was at the Delta counter checking in for my return flight home after spending several hours in a cab enroute to the airport. I watched as an individual walked up to the front of the line and sharply stated to the Delta agent that he had no time to wait in line. He was sweating profusely. He felt his airline status should mean "front of the line." I watched as he berated the young female Delta agent who could do nothing as he unleashed his tirade. He ultimately got in line and, of course, seemed extraordinarily impatient – definitely not winning friends on the airline staff.

After check-in, I watched as he cut to the front of a security line that had been momentarily opened for crew. After wading through security, I arrived at the Delta Sky Club, only to find him front and center in the waiting area. He walked over to pour a glass of wine and spilled the entire bottle all over the floor. He then left it for someone else to it clean up. The final act was upon boarding. He literally pushed three people out of the way to get to his middle seat. Now I did not know this person, but he did have a company logo all over his bags and on the golf shirt he was wearing. I can only imagine how embarrassed his company would have been had they witnessed this behavior.

You represent your company's brand every day. People experience the vision and values of your organization through you and the decisions you make that impact others. Decisions have intended and unintended consequences.

BRINGING IT TO LIFE

◉ **Think:** I don't believe I need to say much more here, as the stories convey the message. Think before you act. Recognize that actions and decisions have consequences. You never really know who is watching! You represent yourself, your family, your company, and the organizations with which you are involved every day. *What do your actions and behaviors say about you?*

◉ **Write Your Story:** *What is your life story? Is it a story you would feel confident in telling? Do you consider daily decisions as part of your future story?* We make decisions early in life and manage those decisions for the rest of our lives. You have the opportunity to choose. Be friends with this person. Avoid that person. Marry this person. Break things off with that person. Partner with this individual. Decline an offer from that individual. Hire this person to be a part of your team. Tell the others "no". Be transparent. Be secretive and judgmental. Tell the truth. Lie and live with the consequences. Decisions have intended and unintended consequences. Make wise choices.

BOTTOM LINE

The things you do when no one is looking are the things that define you.

EXCEPTIONAL. REMARKABLE.
PHENOMENAL. UNUSUAL.
IMPACTFUL. INCOMPARABLE.
WONDERFUL. NOTABLE. MARVELOUS.
LIMITLESS. FANTASTIC. CURIOUS.
OUTSTANDING. DIFFERENTIATED.
OVER-THE-TOP. UNCOMMON.
SINGULAR. SURPRISING. SPECIAL.
ASTONISHING. RARE. UNIQUE.
UNPRECEDENTED. AMAZING. VIVID.
STRONG. MEMORABLE. INCREDIBLE.
AN ANOMALY.

**A DECISION. A CHOICE.
THAT'S EXTRAORDINARY.**

CHAPTER 27

BIG IDEA!
LEADERS ATTRACT LEADERS

"Extraordinary leadership is when a leader is so much for their team that they seek to empower, not overpower. It is when a leader liberates their people to grow personally and professionally."
– Jeremie Kubicek, CEO, GiANT Impact

At some companies, leaders are asked to rank their team on a scale from *one* to *ten* – a *ten* being an outstanding, dynamic, extraordinary, go-to leader; a *one* being an individual with limited leadership capacity. The big idea here is that leaders attract leaders. Place a *six* in a key leadership role and he will attract *fours* and *fives*. Place a *nine* in that same role and he will attract *sevens* and *eights*.

Selecting a leadership team is a critical activity for every organization. Many have made the mistake of promoting *fours* and *fives* up through the organization, instead of counseling them out. The result can be catastrophic, as over time, the cascading effect is an organization full of weak leaders. Some organizations are known for promoting poor performers instead of releasing them to pursue opportunities more aligned with their talents, skills, and leadership capacity. One might hear, "We just need to get them off our team so we can move forward. Even though it's a promotion, at least they are no longer our problem." This is not demonstrative of extraordinary leadership.

The most successful reorganizations are those where intentional thought and care has been put into selecting key business leaders. This eventually cascades down into selecting and creating dynamic teams. When you start with leaders who are *eights, nines*, and *tens* on the scale, you are going to inevitably generate momentum through the big thoughts and ideas that come from these types of leaders. The best leaders want to be surrounded by the best team.

Successful organizational realignments are intentional and leaders of change take the time needed to do a quality job from the beginning. They begin literally top-down, and each level carefully reviews the total talent pool available at the next level. This process continues through the next level of leaders and down through the entire organization. Incredible momentum is generated out of this process, as it is well thought-out and considerate; as opposed to being a shotgun approach solely designed to reach targeted dollar savings or headcount reductions.

One place where I experienced excellence in leaders attracting leaders was in my first role out of college at Ernst & Young (E&Y), LLP. During the interview process, I heard from many friends already employed by E&Y that they truly enjoyed the work and collegial environment. The firm was focused on people development, as opposed to the "churn and burn" mentality found at other competitive firms. When I began working for them, I was immediately enlisted to be a part of several college recruiting teams where I could share my experiences with other prospective new hires. The best hired the best … who hired the best … who hired the best, and so on. To this day, every time we get together for alumni activities, we talk about the people, the partners, the approach, and the customer value delivered – because of the people – during our time at E&Y. E&Y invested heavily in developing its people and this generated tremendous loyalty. Furthermore, several of my E&Y friends are recreating that culture and environment in companies they have founded or companies they are now leading.

BRINGING IT TO LIFE

◉ **Hiring *Tens*:** *What are you personally doing to look for nines and tens versus fives and sixes? Is your recruiting, hiring, and talent management organization set up to identify future organizational leaders and ensure that training and coaching is being provided to prepare them for those roles?*

◉ **Hiring Smarter, Bolder, Stronger:** Sadly, many leaders choose to pass over strong leaders for others who are weaker and more malleable.

They fear looking bad or not as smart as someone else on their team. They also tend to overlook younger, aggressive, talented individuals who, with the proper coaching and mentoring, could soar. *As a side note, age is not indicative of capability or competence.* The key is finding the right mix of backgrounds, personalities, skills, and abilities that balance building capability with delivering value to customers and clients.

◎ **Think Beyond The Standard Interview Questions:** When interviewing candidates for a role, don't simply look for someone to fit a job description. Instead, look for candidates with *stretch* (the ability to go far or wide in the organization) and *runway* (the capacity to grow, develop, change, learn, adapt, and apply). Leaders hire the best talent possible, and in some cases, may need to adjust the defined game plan to ensure a high-octane performer is not lost or misplaced. *What are you doing to ensure that the personal brand qualities of your new hires are being fully exploited within the organization?*

◎ **Talk To Those That Know:** I recently hired a new team member to cover an important section of our business. He and I first met during the interview process. As we were close to making an offer, I requested a number of references from him so that I could get to know him beyond the resume and beyond the interview. I reached out to my network to talk with individuals that I knew had worked with him. Those conversations were tremendously effective in not only validating what I had discerned during the interview, but also in providing me with a starting point in thinking about development opportunities for my new team member. Those conversations were also helpful in framing steps I could take as his new leader to assist him in not only succeeding in the new role on my team, but in pursuing the next level.

◎ **If It's Not Working, Change It . . . Quickly:** If it's not working out, course correct quickly. Despite the best intentions, every hire may not work out. You are going to inevitably make hiring mistakes. Over time, employees within an organization hear about performance issues that are *not* addressed. There is nothing more demotivating to a team than when a leader or organization chooses to ignore or pass around a "performance issue" employee. These situations are also stressful for the leader and often visible to the customer. Address it quickly and move on.

BOTTOM LINE
Surround yourself with the best.

EXCEPTIONAL. REMARKABLE.
PHENOMENAL. UNUSUAL.
IMPACTFUL. INCOMPARABLE.
WONDERFUL. NOTABLE. MARVELOUS.
LIMITLESS. FANTASTIC. CURIOUS.
OUTSTANDING. DIFFERENTIATED.
OVER-THE-TOP. UNCOMMON.
SINGULAR. SURPRISING. SPECIAL.
ASTONISHING. RARE. UNIQUE.
UNPRECEDENTED. AMAZING. VIVID.
STRONG. MEMORABLE. INCREDIBLE.
AN ANOMALY.

**A DECISION. A CHOICE.
THAT'S EXTRAORDINARY.**

CHAPTER 28

BIG IDEA!
PREPARATION PRIMES THE PROCESS

"Extraordinary leadership is the separation of 'what is good enough' to 'what expectations can I surpass with my team, clients, and community.' The key is passion. Passion is what separates the extraordinary executives, athletes, friends, and even family members from the good ones. When you find your passion and have the heart to live it, you will not fail in life."

– Ricky Steele, Chief Development Officer, Hunter Technical Resources

Great leaders build great teams. Like it or not, recruiting new talent is a mainstay of great leadership. It's not a *nice to do*. It's a *must do*. Yet many leaders dislike spending time in the recruitment and interviewing aspects of their role. Certainly, assessing talent is a skill. In working within different organizational environments, different leadership teams, managers and leaders, and under multiple HR strategies, I have found several constants to consider when building out a high-octane team.

Understand the Job – Fully and Completely: If you don't know what you are looking for, you will never find it. It all starts with clearly defining the skills, knowledge, abilities, and cultural characteristics of the individual needed for the role. Then you need to articulate this in a job description or position posting. Many organizations provide a standard job description to a hiring manager once a role is open. As a leader, it is imperative that the job description and associated responsibilities/expectations be clearly defined prior to posting the position. This is not only important in framing up the decision criteria for making a hire, but also for prospective candidates in evaluating their skills versus the position requirements.

Insist on Process Clarity: Before the position is posted, HR and the hiring manager must be on the same page regarding the process. *Who will do what once resumes begin to flow into the pipeline?* Depending on the person, this process will always have unique nuances. *Who screens resumes? Who schedules interviews? Who schedules follow-up interviews? Who will manage feedback from interviews?* Some leaders are very hands-on and wish to drive the entire process – from interview scheduling through decision-making. Some lean into the HR leader to manage the plan and only commit to conducting interviews with the final one or two candidates. Either way, the process must be clear to ensure it runs quickly and efficiently.

Know Your Measurement Criteria: Most interview processes require more than one interview and involve more than one individual on the panel. One way to easily consolidate and review results is to create a table outlining measurement criteria and results by individual. This should directly tie in to criteria defined when initially creating or posting the role. By doing this, you ensure that everyone on the interview panel is on the same page with the hiring decision. This also can assist in supporting the selection process and avoids any ambiguity in decisions.

Get Beyond the Process: The interview is not about an individual nailing the case study method, perfecting their answers using the "STAR" (Situation – Task – Action – Result) format, or achieving a certain score on a personality test. It is truly about finding the right person with the right fit for the role, team, and organization. One mistake often made during an interview is being so focused on the process that one loses site of the individual candidate's natural skills, talents, and personality. The process is essentially a tool that drives conversation and engagement between individuals and establishes a level playing field on which to compare candidates.

Plan to Say "No": The reality is that only one candidate is selected for one job. As a leader, the right thing to do is personally call each of the candidates who were *not* selected to share the news. This is often the most challenging part of the process. Yet it is one of the most crucial, since the way it is handled leaves a lasting impression of the organization and you as a leader. Don't let the interview candidates receive an impersonal HR-system-generated flush letter without first hearing from you.

BRINGING IT TO LIFE

◉ **Own The Process:** Do not rely on HR to be the expert on your business, your team, and your hiring needs. The reality is that your HR business partner or recruiter will be supporting multiple individuals, teams, organizations, processes, and requirements. You must own the process, the job description, the candidate search criteria, the resume review, the interview, and the final decision.

◉ **Own The Communication Plan:** Before reviewing candidates, clearly communicate the role, expectations, interview process, and decision criteria with all members of the interview team. You own the process, therefore you are the expert. Communicate it and ensure that all members of the review panel are aligned on the candidate assessment process.

◉ **Own The Follow-Up:** You lead the interview. You lead the follow-up. Take the time to personally communicate the news to each candidate. If it's good news, this conversation will be the first impression of what working with you will be like. If it's not a positive outcome for the candidate, recognize that your communication could be the final message received from the organization and will leave a lasting impression of the overall experience in working with you and the business.

An informal HR-system-generated flush email or letter is impersonal. Own the final communication.

BOTTOM LINE
Your people decisions affect
the future of the organization.

EXCEPTIONAL. REMARKABLE.
PHENOMENAL. UNUSUAL.
IMPACTFUL. INCOMPARABLE.
WONDERFUL. NOTABLE. MARVELOUS.
LIMITLESS. FANTASTIC. CURIOUS.
OUTSTANDING. DIFFERENTIATED.
OVER-THE-TOP. UNCOMMON.
SINGULAR. SURPRISING. SPECIAL.
ASTONISHING. RARE. UNIQUE.
UNPRECEDENTED. AMAZING. VIVID.
STRONG. MEMORABLE. INCREDIBLE.
AN ANOMALY.

**A DECISION. A CHOICE.
THAT'S EXTRAORDINARY.**

CHAPTER 29

BIG IDEA!
EVALUATION AND SELECTION

"Leaders do not need to add more stress to a situation by lighting
hairs on fire or screaming like a madman during status meetings.
Rather, extraordinary leaders calmly assess problems, make timely
sound decisions, and instill a sense of confidence in team members that
the ship will be steered in the right direction."

– Mike Lenhart, Founder and President, The Getting2Tri Foundation

---

First impressions can make or break you. And, with
few exceptions, first impressions are very likely an
indication of future performance.

I once posted a position and decided to conduct
phone screens prior to scheduling formal interviews
to condense the short-list of candidates. If you are in
sales, business development, consulting, or any other
relationship development role, you know that verbal
communication skills are absolutely critical to success.
This was certainly a critical success factor for my open
role. I called one individual and, before I could even say
hello, he was rattling off his list of wins and successes
and telling me how the job should be done, without
any knowledge of our company or industry. I asked
him what he was interested in doing and found that

he had not done his homework on the role. He knew very little about challenges facing our organization, and then proceeded to try to get my commitment to interview him before hanging up the phone. While I respected his assertiveness, aggressiveness, and success in prior roles, his pushiness would never work with our customers, our team, or our organization. Frankly, it was over-the-top and overly aggressive for an introductory call.

I would never be comfortable putting this type of individual in front of a customer. Relationship-builders are very different than the "slick deal" guy. People buy people and from people. A product can come and go. Sizzle fizzles. The team reflects the leader's brand.

Talent management starts on day one in your role as a leader. That is when you should be considering who would be extraordinary backfill candidates for your role and the roles of your team members. Leaders are always seeking leaders and evaluating talent. Regardless of whether positions are available or not, the best leaders identify, engage with, and develop relationships with top talent. They know that, at some point in the future, an opportunity to work together may arise.

BRINGING IT TO LIFE

Talent evaluation and selection is a critical activity in building the extraordinary team. Here are a few points to consider.

◉ **Character:** *Is this individual trustworthy? Will this person operate with integrity, honesty, and candor, regardless of the situation?*

◉ **Competence:** *Does this individual have the knowledge, skills, and experience to do the job? Does his background enable him to hit the ground running, even with a standard new-role learning curve?*

◉ **Stretch:** *Does this individual have the ability to do more – to move into other roles in the organization – either up or across? What characteristics of the individual make her a utility player? Why do you feel she would be flexible in her movement within the organization? What would be the potential next step for this individual?*

◉ **Runway:** *Does this individual have the capacity or potential to grow, develop, change, learn, adapt, and apply? Will the individual accept coaching and feedback and seek to apply learned concepts?*

◉ **Fit:** *How will this individual "fit" with others on the team? Will he challenge existing processes in a constructive manner? Will she ask questions that lean toward moving the organization forward? How will we operate together and as a team?*

◉ **Culture:** *Does this person add to the culture of the organization by bringing new momentum and energy to the team? Will this person be a catalyst for positive momentum?*

◉ **Communication:** Communication is the glue that keeps an organization running, growing, and evolving. It is often a key foundation element to a winning partnership. *Is the individual clear and succinct in communication? Does the individual talk in circles, talk too much, or talk over others versus answering the question? Would you feel comfortable placing this person in front of a customer?*

◉ **Creativity:** While many roles would not necessarily require creativity, every role has some aspect that could benefit from it. *Would this individual bring new ideas, new process thinking, new engagement concepts, or new relationships to the organization that did not exist in the past? Would this individual challenge our team's creative curiosity?*

BOTTOM LINE
Be specific. Evaluate and select strategically.

CHAPTER 30

BIG IDEA!
ENGAGE, INVEST, RETAIN

"Extraordinary leadership is the ability to describe reality and then to give hope. It is the ability to be realistic in your assessment of today and work with hope to build a better tomorrow. Leaders know that challenges are a passing thing – that a new day will come and that day will shine even brighter. We are all tempted daily to turn back, but leaders with hope keep going to bring about the good in the world."

– David Findley, Vice President of Sales, Randstad Engineering

The dust is settling after a major organizational change. The company has right-sized and reorganized. New commitments have been made to move forward. Leadership roles are filled. Calls are being made. Orders are being placed. Inventories are being replenished. Product is being delivered. Even though the all-clear siren has sounded, people are still faced with new challenges from a major organizational restructure.

Employees will no doubt find themselves standing in a very different place than where they started. The team now has fewer resources at their disposal. Employees are called on to do more with less in the name of cost savings and growth. What was old is no longer, and the new looks unfamiliar. Titles and org charts are different. Some people start to look around for different opportunities, questioning the new direction and the change that surrounds them.

At the end of the day, it's all about positive employee retention. While some degree of turnover is good and should be expected as the bar is continually raised, strong leaders want to minimize the unwanted attrition that occurs within a business. When businesses undergo major organizational change through mergers, acquisitions, takeovers, or economic downturns, employees are stressed and seek consistency in operating rhythm and structure.

You, as the leader, must quickly survey and understand the landscape, then take steps to ensure that you retain your top talent.

BRINGING IT TO LIFE

◎ **Start With Communication:** You can never communicate enough when it comes to engaging employees. Just as in real estate, where it's all about *location, location, location*, keeping employees connected and engaged to the workplace is all about *communication, communication, communication*. Employees want to feel connected. They want to feel "in the know." They want to feel as if they have a say, and that their opinion is valued. Ask questions. Solicit feedback. The productivity and process improvements you discover may be extraordinary.

◉ **Employee Ownership:** Create new opportunities for employees. Perhaps they can play a role on new projects or in departments where they typically would not have had much interaction. Ask yourself what you can do to engage developing talent while giving them exposure to other aspects of the business. Recognize that the answer may very well be different for each person. Customize your engagement activities. One size does not fit all in this instance.

◉ **Team-Building:** Create team-building opportunities. Not ropes courses, but rather opportunities where employees have a chance to get to know each other better and build relationships with one another, thus becoming more engaged with each other. Increased engagement with the employer is a natural by-product of this process. As employees engage more with one another, work can become less like work and more like fun or family.

◉ **Smart Risk-Taking:** Getting employees to re-engage often means getting them to step outside of their comfort zone and take risks. Allow for failure and use it as a coaching opportunity. Reward the new ideas.

◉ **Executive Coaching:** Hire an executive coach for those employees with significant stretch and runway. Executive coaching was once viewed as a tool only to be used to help those people who needed "extra help" to be successful. Or for those who were being given one final chance to figure it out. Today, however, the momentum has shifted and suddenly it's clearly acceptable to have a coach. In fact, it's a good thing if your company is making an investment in your employee's development by allowing them the opportunity to work with an executive coach. When an employee sees the company making this kind of investment, he or she will recognize the inherent reward and tag of being considered high potential, and their engagement increases.

BOTTOM LINE

Employee engagement is a top people priority.

CHAPTER 31

BIG IDEA!
EXTRAORDINARY OPPORTUNITY, UNEXPECTED TIMING

"Extraordinary leadership is inspiring greatness in those around you in pursuit of a common vision. It is uniting disparate talents around a common mission. It is utilizing influence to open doors and remove obstacles."

– Raymond King, CEO, Zoo Atlanta

It was the P-E-R-F-E-C-T role. But I had only been in my current job for ten months, so the answer was "no." I missed an extraordinary opportunity because I had not been in my role for 18 months.

It is frequently a policy within organizations that one must stay in a given role for a set period of time. *But what if the perfect role opens up for one of your team members? Are you going to tell them "no" and not support their pursuit of the opportunity? What if the role is an absolute perfect career next step or promotion? Does this change anything?*

I certainly understand the argument that it takes a solid 12-24 months for an individual to acclimate to a new role, ramp up, and deliver results. I also recognize the need to ensure that the team and the organization do not garner the "revolving door" reputation. *But if the alternative is frustration and discontent in a top performer, is it worth it? If the alternative is a high-octane performer considering looking outside the company due to this rule, is it worth it? As a leader, isn't it your responsibility to continue to promote top talent to drive new momentum in the organization?* Dynamic tension for sure.

My unwritten rule is that it takes 12 months for a team member to achieve qualitative and quantitative business results. But regardless of timing, I will always support my team members in pursuing their career goals, aspirational positions, promotions, and lateral skill-building roles. I will also never hold back an employee because of a perceived lack of backfill candidates. I am failing as their leader if I am not always thinking of top talent that could backfill my own role as well as other roles on my team.

As the saying goes, "fate rarely calls upon us at the moment of our choosing"!

BRINGING IT TO LIFE

◉ **Set Expectations Early:** If there is a rule, there is a rule. Communicate it so your team knows what to expect. And if you choose to make an exception, know that others will see it and could expect the same. Also, maintain a team talent management file where you document the status of each team member in their career development process and potential backfill candidates for each person. This is a collaborative, ongoing discussion with each team member as you *lean into them* to identify top talent backfills for their positions. Review the succession planning content monthly with each team member, so that they are a part of ensuring the ongoing growth and stability of your organization.

◎ **Be Flexible:** What if it is the right opportunity, the right skill set, the right person, and the right level in the organization? This could be the perfect opportunity. The perfect role. And even though it might be out of process, it could benefit the team member and you in the long run. Plus you can then recruit the next extraordinary leader to join the team!

◎ **Craft A 30-60-90-day Plan:** One way you can help your team members effectively pursue their next career step is to help each of them craft a 30-60-90-day plan. Consider a framework that consists of buckets of activities for *People Development, Process Improvement, Customer Engagement,* and *Organizational Effectiveness.* Define activities that fit into 30-60-90 day periods. Think of the 30-day period as the *Learn/Assess* phase. The 60-day period as the *Analyze/Prioritize* phase. And the 90-day period as the *Execute/Lead Change* phase. This helps to ensure that there is a clear definition of approach, activities, and deliverables during the ramp-up into the new role. This tool is also useful as a communication platform between employee and leader to ensure that the employee's work efforts are aligned with the leader's concept for the role. At the end of the day, both want to be speaking the same language and pursuing the same organizational vision. It is also imperative that success metrics are aligned. In a coaching and mentoring capacity, assisting in developing a 30-60-90-day plan can be of immense value. This framework demonstrates that an individual has thought about the role, the team, the expectations, and the future state in which the new role operates. It demonstrates a commitment to getting up to speed quickly and making a measurable impact early and often.

BOTTOM LINE

There is no richer reward than seeing your team members succeed, progress, and achieve.

CHAPTER 32

BIG IDEA!
TEAM MOMENTUM

"Extraordinary leadership is having fearless drive
and commitment to succeed."
– Tracy Lawrence, Country Music Singer and Songwriter

Momentum is critical to maintaining a motivated team. Small wins create momentum. New tools, new team members, new investments, and new processes create momentum. Momentum fuels the team to achieve more. It builds on the framework established by wins – both big and small – and by overcoming challenges. Momentum is a fascinating concept. It is essential to organizational growth, team growth, and personal growth. Momentum drives growth, enables change, and delivers unexpected results.

Consider the world of business development. In an environment of long cycle time business partner deals, every bit of momentum is absolutely invaluable and critical to maintaining an engaged team. Business development is making cold calls. It is attempting every creative method possible to open a door to create a conversation. It is receiving and dealing with the "not interested" phone calls and the "we've gone with your competitor" emails. It is giving it your all, only to be beaten on price. Business development requires consistently delivering a can-do, make-it-happen, believe-in-yourself, self-starter, positive attitude to the team. Leveraging momentum is important.

Being able to build upon that momentum is huge. When a team member or colleague accomplishes a major milestone in a project, celebrate it, recognize it, and share it. This builds momentum. Act quickly to ensure that you focus your energy on achieving next steps, as these moments of positive momentum may not last long. Conversely, when someone loses a big deal to the competition, ensure that you immediately debrief and evaluate together as to why this occurred. What went well and what needs to be done differently next time? Sometimes the most valuable lessons are, in fact, learned from losses versus wins, as we discussed in previous chapters. When, as a leader, you can translate a negative event into positive team momentum, you win. And so does your team.

BRINGING IT TO LIFE

◉ **Build:** As a leader, there is no better momentum driver than a highly motivated team. In fact, team momentum may be the ultimate catalyst for organizational growth and achievement. Recognize

it. Embrace it. And leverage it fully into fuel
for pushing the team to raise the bar. Energy is
contagious and your team undoubtedly has
high-octane performers who bring positive energy
to every project, initiative, and pursuit. These
are your go-to team members; the ones that have
extensive capacity and are able to deliver results
quickly. Team momentum will translate into
positive growth for the organization. Recruit these
individuals. Invest in these individuals. Promote
these individuals. And don't forget to celebrate
their successes along the way.

◉ **Assess:** Leaders make time to step back and
assess *drivers* of team momentum. It is imperative
that you identify what fuels the team. *What is it
that drives positive forward momentum for each team
member individually, and for the team collectively? Is it
rewards and recognition? Is it a high-touch, collaborative,
communicative environment? Is it seeing others on
the team achieving success and seeing those successes
celebrated? Is it being asked to take on more and owning
the outcome of larger initiatives?* Ask yourself, *"What
drives negative team momentum?"* Is it a lack of support
from other groups in the organization? Is it internal red
tape and politics? Is it a flawed business strategy, vision,
and model for growth?* When you recognize what
drives and destroys team momentum, you can
work toward reinforcing the elements that drive

positive momentum, while limiting those that destroy momentum.

◉ **Persist:** The surest way to fail is to quit. Often a lack of business support, limited resources, and the constantly changing business requirements landscape seem to be the only constants. It's easy to get frustrated. Be persistent. The small wins will start to add up. They will soon become larger wins and ultimately lead to the momentum needed to get through major activities, tasks, and deliverables. Don't stop to look behind you. Just keep running.

BOTTOM LINE

Team results translates into
organizational momentum.

CHAPTER 33

BIG IDEA!
ORGANIZATIONAL MOMENTUM

"Extraordinary leadership is forward-thinking; passionate; optimistic.
Extraordinary leadership empowers others to meet the challenges of
whatever enterprise they may be a part of – personal or professional.
Extraordinary leaders ensure that each member of their team is growing,
humanely, as an individual. In the end, they are becoming leaders
themselves by helping others to do the same."

– Bob Watson, Executive Director, 21st Century Leaders

Positive organizational momentum may be triggered by many things: a new leader, a new brand launch, a new organizational structure, a new acquisition or divestiture, a new technology, a new vision, or a new strategy for execution.

I have experienced the organizational momentum concept play out several times in my career. In the late 1990s, I joined a niche strategy consulting firm in a supply chain e-commerce leadership role. This organization hit the market in a big way, providing services to existing businesses and start-ups. It did an amazing job of attracting the absolute best industry leaders. We were signing new deals left and right. The office quickly became too small. We were growing exponentially. Positive momentum was tangible. You could feel it and see it in the excitement that was representative in the office, the community, and with our customers. Positive momentum was initiated by a market that was fueling start-ups, new investments in e-commerce, and customers looking to fully harness the power of the internet. The momentum was further fueled by the infusion of top industry thought-leaders working in an environment that encouraged a *ready-fire-aim* strategy of delivering results.

Then the momentum shifted ... in the opposite direction. The internet bubble burst and the stock market crashed. New start-ups were no longer receiving funding. The venture capital faucet quickly shut off. Our organization, which was spending money furiously, quickly found itself in an unsustainable business situation. This situation similarly played out for many firms. The customer landscape changed while firms were still over-spending on operating expenses. Negative momentum took over and destroyed businesses, careers, and substantial investment capital. Like dominos collapsing onto one another, businesses began to fail.

Positive momentum is often found in a new brand launch versus a line extension; in a new organization structure versus an organizational tweak; or in a new leader. What my former company failed to do, like many other organizations, was to *adapt* to overwhelmingly negative market momentum that quickly knocked it off its narrow base of business.

Consider the launch of a new product line. Much fanfare, celebration, and advertising goes into the product launch. And, over time, without a sustained brand-building investment and/or follow-through that triggers trial, growth and evolution, a new brand can quickly decline. It can painfully wilt under the weight of bloated corporate and investor expectations. Investment wanes. Strategies change. Ultimately, brand objectives are repositioned with investment moving on to the next new brand idea.

Positive organization momentum is often created as part of business reorganization. I have played significant roles in multiple, major enterprise-wide reorganizations. One in particular shook things up and created a new level of positive momentum that flowed through the entire business. It placed the right people in the right roles and tore down artificial organizational barriers and silos. It opened up communication channels between teams and individuals that never existed prior to the change. It introduced new tools, techniques, strategies, and approaches for solving customer business problems. It encouraged new ideas and creative thinking – with the customer front and center. The results were clearly evident in people, processes, and technology functions. There was a decrease in the time it took to get things done. An increase in the overall culture vibe across the organization. A new sense of collaboration. Positive feedback from customers. And improved business results. Positive organizational momentum was triggered through change.

The key is triggering events that create and sustain momentum. *What actions can you take as the leader to continue to fuel positive organizational momentum?*

BRINGING IT TO LIFE

◉ **Embrace "New":** There is no more powerful fuel for momentum than introducing something new. Introducing a new leader. A new organizational structure. A new brand. New packaging and messaging. A new marketing and advertising campaign. A new acquisition. A new investment. Most people fear change and fear having to learn something new. Yet that something new can prove to be the catalyst for growth, development, change, and evolution for an entire organization. It is also important to recognize that new does not mean making small changes to something old, something that exists, or something that could be modified. New is new. *What are you doing that is new; that is challenging the system thinking and breaking the mold?*

◉ **Assess:** Before introducing new concepts and ideas to the organization, assess what is working and what areas require change. *Where can you build on team wins across the organization?* Take time to step back and assess drivers of organizational momentum. *Is it people, process, brand, or* *customer-driven momentum? What fuels the organization? What are the drivers of positive forward momentum? What drives negative organizational momentum? Is it lack of support from other groups in the organization? Is it internal red tape and politics? Is it a flawed business strategy, vision, and model for growth?* When you recognize what drives and destroys an organization's momentum, you can work toward reinforcing the elements that drive positive momentum while limiting those that destroy it. *Personal* momentum fuels *team* momentum which fuels *organizational* momentum.

◉ **Persist:** The organization will naturally conspire to revert to the *old* and to veer away from accepting change. As the leader, leverage positive team momentum to build overall organizational momentum. Communicate the wins and the linkage between the wins and the vision and strategies set forth by the organization. As the leader, persistence will be your greatest value, and therefore, your asset to ensure that new ideas are accepted and become the new standard, thereby driving organizational momentum. Persistence pays off.

BOTTOM LINE

Organizational momentum translates into customer momentum and marketplace success.

EXCEPTIONAL. REMARKABLE.
PHENOMENAL. UNUSUAL.
IMPACTFUL. INCOMPARABLE.
WONDERFUL. NOTABLE. MARVELOUS.
LIMITLESS. FANTASTIC. CURIOUS.
OUTSTANDING. DIFFERENTIATED.
OVER-THE-TOP. UNCOMMON.
SINGULAR. SURPRISING. SPECIAL.
ASTONISHING. RARE. UNIQUE.
UNPRECEDENTED. AMAZING. VIVID.
STRONG. MEMORABLE. INCREDIBLE.
AN ANOMALY.

**A DECISION. A CHOICE.
THAT'S EXTRAORDINARY.**

CHAPTER 34

BIG IDEA!
BLOCKING AND TACKLING

"The will to win is worthless, unless you have the will to prepare.
Extraordinary leadership is demonstrating actions that speak so loud that
there is no need to hear what you say."

– Dan Reeves, Head Football Coach, National Football League

Many people don't recognize that they drop the ball on the little things. They forget the basics and only a few people are fanatical about the details. Many people make excuses for not executing on action-items and follow-up. And very few have a *blocking and tackling* routine.

I recently had an initial discovery meeting with a customer, and before we had moved beyond names and roles, the customer said, "I just need to know that you will be responsive. I need to know that you will return my calls and at least be somewhat proactive in bringing new ideas to our partnership." I should have been surprised, but since this was the fourth time I had heard this from a prospect in many months, it became more of a rallying cry for me and my team. What this customer was asking for was the basics. Something they felt was clearly missing from our primary competitor.

Many individuals looking to initiate and grow winning partnerships falter on day one by simply failing to block and tackle. They fail to follow-through on commitments. They fail to follow-up after meetings with action items, thank you notes, or even memorable gifts. At the end of the day, partnerships are founded on the basics. Blocking and tackling gets things done. It moves the relationship forward. It solves problems that are inherent with all new relationships. It instills a foundation of trust. Trust is something that cannot be established through words, but rather through actions, behaviors, and interactions.

Relationships begin and end through a simple concept called *listening* (another blocking and tackling fundamental we covered earlier in the book). For those fortunate enough to actually hear what a customer or prospect is requesting, and then ensuring that steps are taken to address those items, will find that their relationship will get off to a fast start.

At the same time, blocking and tackling does not end once a contract has been signed or a project is complete. *How will you ensure that the level of customer engagement continues to grow as the partnership evolves?* The customer needs a partner for today, tomorrow, and the future. If you don't have a strong customer management team, your partnerships will be short-lived, and will quickly erode the organization's brand.

BRINGING IT TO LIFE

◉ **Follow-Up And Follow-Through:** After each and every meeting, distribute meeting notes in a structured format. Highlight action items and explain details regarding the next proposed or confirmed interaction. Write personal thank you notes to each and every individual with whom you meet. This small activity goes immensely further than anything your competition will do. The art of writing thank you notes is almost extinct ... which is exactly why they are so powerful. Interestingly, my church maintains a routine whereby staff members write weekly thank you notes to volunteers recognizing extraordinary efforts. It's unique. It's different. It's special. And it's a small way to send a powerful, appreciative message.

◉ **Project Management 101:** Selling and delivering a product or service is founded on project management fundamentals. There is discovery, solution design, a build or deploy with the customer, and a hand-off to account management. The best business partnership teams understand these concepts and think of every new prospect from the perspective of a project. Customers appreciate communication and there are times when *over-communication* is a plus.

◉ **Process Check:** It's pretty simple to confirm this concept. Just think about the solution-providers, contractors, and consultants you work with who are excellent at blocking and tackling. They engage, deliver, follow-through, and follow-up. Think about travel companies, airlines, hotels, online retailers, consulting partners, or software/hardware providers. You notice when they do things right. All it takes is one bad experience and a customer can quickly change perception and direction. It comes down to the little things – the things that are often discarded or pushed to the side in an effort to move faster, or that get dropped due to multiple competing priorities. The things that set you apart. That differentiate you.

BOTTOM LINE

Top teams win by overachieving on the basics.

CHAPTER 35

BIG IDEA!
ON-TIME, IN-FULL (OTIF)

"Extraordinary leadership is knowing how to invest your hours
wisely – and encouraging everyone around you to do the same. How we
invest our hours determines whether we stagnate or thrive."

– Laura Vanderkam, Author of *What the Most Successful
People Do Before Breakfast* (2012),
All The Money In The World (2012), and *168 Hours* (2010)

If you are a supply chain guru, you probably recognize the phrase "On-Time, In-Full" or OTIF as it is a metric frequently used by suppliers to measure success at delivering exactly what the customer ordered on the day it was supposed to be delivered.

For example, a retailer places an order for product from a consumer goods supplier. The supplier either does or does not deliver the order on the date assigned, and the order either is or is not completed. The results feed into a derived metric that ensures focus on process excellence with a customer. The metric: "On-Time, In-Full."

When I read this phrase, I also think about being *on-time* and contributing *in-full* to the day-to-day operations of the business and the after-hour contributions to community and philanthropic endeavors. This means showing up on time for scheduled meetings. Arriving early for events. Following up with stakeholders in the timeframe prescribed and with the requested content. Preparing and doing homework prior to a meeting or working session in order to contribute in-full. Offering to take notes, follow-up, and schedule the next meeting or working session. Bringing my full self – knowledge, insights, energy, focus, and ideas – to a team meeting, working session, or community activity. Leaving my Blackberry in the case and my laptop closed during meetings. All this and more is the *leader* version of OTIF – being on-time and contributing in-full.

Many organizations, teams, and individuals would not receive a high or favorable OTIF score if we used it to gauge individual contribution or engagement. The unintended consequences of ignoring this simple measure are significant.

Research shows that 11 million meetings occur in the U.S. every day, and most professionals attend nearly 62 meetings per month (source: *Infocomm*). That is a lot of meetings. These same professionals admit that they regularly: daydream (91%), miss meetings (96%), miss parts of meetings (95%), bring other work to meetings (73%), and occasionally doze off during meeting (39%). Certainly not OTIF behavior!

BRINGING IT TO LIFE

◉ **On-Time, Every-Time:** Begin and end on-time. It sounds simple, and yet for some strange reason this principle is not regularly followed. *Start on-time. End on-time.* It is frequently the case that we want to give latecomers a few extra minutes to dial-in, even though others have made it a point to be on time. Go ahead, start the meeting and allow others to be late. Do not rehash what has already been covered. They can find time after the meeting to pick up what they have missed. Acknowledge the value of others' time by being on-time. *How are you doing on this? Do you start and end your meetings on-time? Do you manage scope creep (uncontrolled changes in a project's scope during the meeting) so that you have your best shot at accomplishing the set agenda within the time scheduled? If you are going to run out of time, do you schedule a follow-up discussion?*

◉ **When You Commit, Make It Fit:** It had been on my calendar for a month. I had a half-day working session at noon in New York City with one of our entertainment business partners. I decided to fit in a second meeting that morning which, if all worked *perfectly,* would still allow me to make it into the city in time for the partner meeting. *Perfectly* didn't work. I was 45 minutes late. My being late, after committing to being there at a specific date and time, was understandably perceived as rude. Unfortunately, the perception was that my time was more valuable, and that I had placed a higher priority on spending time with another group. Even worse, one of my team members had established the agenda and set it up for me to kickoff. This incident was an important lesson learned, and one that was frustrating, as it could have easily been avoided. When you commit, make sure it fits your calendar. Narrow the focus and truly be on-time, every-time. Juggling priorities can be fun and enjoyable, as long as you are not shortchanging the relationship. Failing to give your full self to each priority is a mark of failure as a leader.

◉ **Silence It. Ignore It. Leave It:** It is not easy to leave your cell phone tucked away during a meeting. It is not easy ignoring emails and calls while participating in a workshop. It is not easy to ignore that *new mail* notification on the bottom of your laptop screen while typing notes during a meeting. I have certainly been guilty of multi-tasking in meetings, and yet I still find it exceedingly frustrating when others pull this act on me. I have come to appreciate when others are fully engaged in meetings. So much more gets accomplished, so many more ideas are shared, and so many more relationships are moved to the next level. Respect of others is gained by giving your full energy and attention. What's the point of attending a meeting if all you are going to do is email? Silence it … ignore it … or just leave it in your office. Choose to check out in meetings and you will lose credibility. Choose to do your emails while others are working through a deliverable and risk losing the respect of your colleagues. Do it often enough and you become the brunt of jokes and lowered engagement expectations. All of this serves as a major hit to the value of your personal brand. Not extraordinary.

◉ **Score Yourself:** *If you were going to rank yourself on the OTIF scale from 1 to 10, where would you fit? Are you a 1: always late, typically unprepared, disengaged, or distracted? Or a 10: always early or on-time, prepared, and fully actively engaged? How would you score the members of your team? How would you score the team as a whole? Even better, how would you score the organizational culture for OTIF as an expectation?*

BOTTOM LINE
OTIF or lose it.

EXCEPTIONAL. REMARKABLE.
PHENOMENAL. UNUSUAL.
IMPACTFUL. INCOMPARABLE.
WONDERFUL. NOTABLE. MARVELOUS.
LIMITLESS. FANTASTIC. CURIOUS.
OUTSTANDING. DIFFERENTIATED.
OVER-THE-TOP. UNCOMMON.
SINGULAR. SURPRISING. SPECIAL.
ASTONISHING. RARE. UNIQUE.
UNPRECEDENTED. AMAZING. VIVID.
STRONG. MEMORABLE. INCREDIBLE.
AN ANOMALY.

**A DECISION. A CHOICE.
THAT'S EXTRAORDINARY.**

CHAPTER 36

BIG IDEA!
A FRESH SET OF EYES

"Extraordinary leadership is leadership that inspires passion and confidence; brings together the talents of a diverse group of people into a productive and highly successful team; and motivates thoughtful action. Extraordinary leaders are unafraid to take bold stands, to get in front of their followers to set courageous direction, and to take on the status quo. Through their clear vision, unyielding commitment to excellence, and deep care and concern for those they lead, these leaders make a lasting and significant positive difference in their organizations and the broader communities in which they interact."

– Joe Seivold, Headmaster, Berkeley Preparatory School

A billion-dollar spacecraft. A multimillion-dollar payload. A multinational crew of astronauts. And yet, one of the most important final close-out activities on the pad before the space shuttle could launch, was a very manual, yet highly important activity called the *pad walk-down*. I worked for NASA in Space Shuttle Operations for three years while at Georgia Tech. During that time I had the opportunity to co-lead a number of orbiter move, launch, and space shuttle processing operations.

Every task, project, and activity associated with processing the shuttle for flight involved multiple *sets of eyes* or quality assurance sign-offs to ensure that the work had not only been completed, but had been completed per specs outlined in detailed manuals. Prior to launch, a final Foreign Object Debris (FOD) team consisting of a cross-functional team of individuals would start at the top of launch pad 39-A or 39-B and walk down the entire structure to collect anything that could damage the shuttle tiles during launch. The value of the cross-functional FOD walk-down team was that a fresh set of eyes could check every aspect of the pad structure. The idea was that things that could easily be missed by someone working routinely on the structure. However, those same things would stick out to others who applied a fresh look at the environment.

The same principle applies in any business environment. One of my team members recently put together a customer presentation and asked for feedback on the content, structure, and approach. I printed the slides, taped them to a whiteboard, and invited another team member to join us in reviewing them and providing feedback. We reordered. We restructured. We added. We subtracted. We asked many questions ... all in the name of raising the bar. The finished product was a remarkable success. The initial pitch was good, and could have easily been the final customer presentation. But, by asking for a fresh set of eyes to review, critique, and provide additional perspective, the presentation and associated content went from great to extraordinary.

In another case, our team had defined 6-8 major customer opportunities in our channel that could lead to extraordinary win-win partnerships. The customer would win by finding millions of dollars in incremental revenue. We would win by achieving new channel penetration, a new exclusive relationship, and expansion of our product's availability to shoppers preferring our brands. In defining the *big idea*, we had exhausted all of our *known* content sources. We decided to pull together a cross-functional group for an ideation session. This diverse group that spanned different channels, roles and business areas, provided new and different insights. They looked at the opportunities and applied a new set of creative thinking to re-set, grow, and/or further develop the big ideas.

The results from just a handful of these one hour ideation sessions were eye-opening. New assets were brought to the table – assets that our team had previously not been aware of. New ideas and concepts were suggested – ones that were working well in other channels, but had not been applied in ours. A fresh set of eyes completely changed our perspective, our big ideas, and the resulting proposals to the prospect leadership.

BRINGING IT TO LIFE

◉ **Define Where It Would Help:** Let's face it. We don't need any more unwanted or unrequested opinions on our business. As a former manager once said, "Opinions are like noses. Everybody has one and they all smell!" At the same time, strategically, a fresh set of eyes can initiate momentum around a project, pursuit, or new idea. There are many smart and talented individuals in large organizations, and most people love to be asked for their opinions and ideas. *Can you identify an area where having a fresh perspective may help?*

◉ **Exchange Value:** The key to rewarding a fresh set of eyes is acknowledging them for participation. This starts and ends with providing updates on the end result. When individuals offer input and advice, the best exchange of value is demonstrating that their ideas have been integrated and utilized. This makes them more likely to help again in the future. *Do you circle back and provide updates to those individuals who help you? What are you doing to make them feel involved and appreciated?*

◉ **Fuel Creativity:** For process, financial, and people-oriented leaders, there is immense value in bringing creativity to the table in defining solutions. Depending on your audience, creativity and out-of-the-box thinking may be the key that opens the proverbial relationship lock and leads to a partnership centered on a balance of financials, partnership hand-offs, and creative concepts. *What are you doing to fuel or bring creativity to the table?*

◉ **Reach Out:** Most people enjoy being invited to provide input, ideas, insights, or an opinion – especially when there is the opportunity to contribute to something new and different. Reach out. Engage. Just ask. You will be surprised at the positive level of interest and response you receive.

BOTTOM LINE

With fresh eyes, ideas fly.

EXCEPTIONAL. REMARKABLE.
PHENOMENAL. UNUSUAL.
IMPACTFUL. INCOMPARABLE.
WONDERFUL. NOTABLE. MARVELOUS.
LIMITLESS. FANTASTIC. CURIOUS.
OUTSTANDING. DIFFERENTIATED.
OVER-THE-TOP. UNCOMMON.
SINGULAR. SURPRISING. SPECIAL.
ASTONISHING. RARE. UNIQUE.
UNPRECEDENTED. AMAZING. VIVID.
STRONG. MEMORABLE. INCREDIBLE.
AN ANOMALY.

**A DECISION. A CHOICE.
THAT'S EXTRAORDINARY.**

CHAPTER 37

BIG IDEA!
MAKE IT WORK. MAKE IT BETTER. MAKE IT BEST.

"Being an extraordinary leader is found in linking the word 'extra' to the word 'ordinary.' The extra passion, the extra curiosity, the extra time put towards execution, the extra time put towards helping others, and even the extra time asking for help from others. All those little extras combined, elevate you to a level of success where others will want to follow."

– Kate Atwood, Executive Director, Arby's Foundation

Make it work. Make it better. Make it best. This concept is a great three-step approach to any new challenge, and easily translates into a winning partnership strategy.

Make it work. Step one in developing successful partnerships is getting off to a *fast start*. Nothing is perfect on day one, and yet the new partnership needs momentum and early wins to ensure long-term permanence. Making it work means getting something to market quickly. It means establishing a framework on which the partnership can be built; on which the partnership can be sustained; and on which the partnership can learn and evolve. It means pushing aside all of the reasons why something cannot work, or all of the reasons that we cannot reach 100% on week one. It means recognizing that getting in-market together, executing together, and winning together in at least a percentage of the business is a starting point ... and something that can be built upon.

This played out recently with a customer that asked my team to deliver products through a channel that we typically did not utilize. They were only interested in a handful of specific products and not our full portfolio. We flexed to meet the alternate supply chain method and worked through getting the customer only the products they needed without over-selling additional options. We knew that if we could just make the relationship hand-offs work, other business would potentially develop in the future.

Make it better. Step two in the process means taking the foundation that has been built and making it more efficient, making it stronger, and building onto the products, capabilities, and solutions that are being delivered via the partnership. It could also mean improving the hand-offs that take place in any partnership. In another of my customer experiences, we evaluated and selected products and packages for a customer looking to expand their overall business offering. We re-evaluated our route to market and how we were collaborating in the supply chain and order management space to fit with the model desired by the customer. A partnership was in place, and very quickly, over time, progressed from transactional partnership to integrated relationship based on our collaboration.

Make it best. Step three. In an ideal world, a partnership evolves over time in an upward, positive trajectory. It may occasionally hit plateaus and then continue to get stronger, sharper, and ever more productive and efficient. This final step, making it best, is what I remember as the old *continuous improvement* process or methodology I learned in management consulting. Making it best is not a one-time tweak or a one-time strategic decision. Making it best means operating in a cadence that involves open, trust-based communication. It means collaborating up and down the chain of partnership hand-offs. It means bringing a true passion for the business and desire to win. It means complete leadership alignment between organizations.

BRINGING IT TO LIFE

◉ **Manage Expectations Internally:** Your internal management may not understand why you are short-selling the initial partnership options in order to *make it work*. Recognize that you may need to manage internal expectations regarding the strategy to win long-term, and that the short-term solution may be the *make it work* solution.

◉ **Formalize Process For Evaluation And Measurement:** This happens by establishing a process, from day one, that provides for continuous measurement, evaluation, and flexibility to change course in order to achieve the desired vision for winning together. This should be built into every business partnership. Clearly define at the initial partnership meeting the desire to evaluate and tweak monthly, quarterly, or at whatever frequency is desired by the customer. This builds trust and a sense that we are in it to win together – that we are passionate about long-term invested partnerships.

◉ **Clarify The Win And Get The Right People On The Team:** Making it best means that everyone understands the vision for a winning partnership. Ensures that everyone understands how success is measured up and down the chain of involved parties on the partnership teams. Ensures that trust is inherent in the day-to-day business, and that the right people are on the team to enable things to move quickly and efficiently across organizations. It also means that additional tweaks, changes, and leaps of partnership faith that take the relationship to the next level are going to be accepted. It is these things that change markets and change dynamics in an industry. It is these things that transform an organization and inherent partnerships from *operating* to *accelerating*.

BOTTOM LINE

Get it working. Invest in making it better.
Tweak to make it best.

CHAPTER 38

BIG IDEA!
DIFFERENTIATED APPROACH

"Extraordinary leadership is being able to motivate people to willingly and eagerly follow you down a path that may not be easy or obvious. People will believe in and trust an extraordinary leader. They will give the leader the benefit of the doubt. Without that trust it would be impossible for the leader to pursue their visionary path forward."

– Bill Franks, Chief Analytics Officer, Teradata and
Author of *Taming The Data Tidal Wave*

To win with customers others are pursuing, we must do things our competition is not doing.

Beyond unique product characteristics, previous solution delivery experience, and subject matter expertise in an industry, the approach you take to building partnerships is one of the most unique methods by which you can differentiate yourself versus the competition. As discussed earlier, competing on price alone is not a winning proposition. To win with partners, when your solution offerings are similar to the competition, you must bring more to the table. You must approach the partnership differently and in a way that appeals to the strategies, plans, and priorities of the customer. You must transform from a product or service provider to a *solution provider*. You must solve your customer's problems and help them to overcome business challenges.

Once you understand your customer's business priorities, you can map products, services, and capabilities to each as a solution to the customer's problem. The conversation centers on how you partner around solving those problems – together – versus centering the conversation on a single brand, product, package, or point solution.

During my consulting days, we leveraged a solution-selling approach that combined product, service, and capability knowledge with skills as a solution to solve major corporate challenges. The same could be done by a product company. In consulting, we approached every opportunity with a solution-selling approach versus a product approach. Why not do the same for a product or service? Begin by defining the key business challenges facing your customer. Then align your assets, products, services, and capabilities against solving those problems. The final piece is demonstrating why your people are the right ones to deliver the solutions (see earlier chapters on hiring the right talent) and why it makes sense to move forward now (a sense of urgency).

When you approach partnerships with an extraordinary focus on the customer, the customer expects a partnership with an extraordinary focus on them. Simple concept.

BRINGING IT TO LIFE

◙ **What's Unique In Your Approach?:** *What does your organization do, make, or deliver that is unique? How is it differentiated from the competition? What could you be doing that is different or unique – something you are not doing today in solving your customer's business problems? How can you translate brand, product, package, and/or service value to solutions that solve your customers' problems?* The key to differentiated action is to first understand the current state and allow for creativity and new ideas to infiltrate the strategy definition process for the organization.

◙ **Act, Refine, Act:** There is no way to determine if your actions will have the desired end-goal affect unless you try. Test. Make change and measure. The key is to evaluate and refine based on results, and then reinvest. Over time, it becomes a cycle that ensures that fresh ideas and new methods are constantly evaluated, tested, and evaluated again as the possible next *big thing*.

BOTTOM LINE

Be distinct or be extinct.

EXCEPTIONAL. REMARKABLE.
PHENOMENAL. UNUSUAL.
IMPACTFUL. INCOMPARABLE.
WONDERFUL. NOTABLE. MARVELOUS.
LIMITLESS. FANTASTIC. CURIOUS.
OUTSTANDING. DIFFERENTIATED.
OVER-THE-TOP. UNCOMMON.
SINGULAR. SURPRISING. SPECIAL.
ASTONISHING. RARE. UNIQUE.
UNPRECEDENTED. AMAZING. VIVID.
STRONG. MEMORABLE. INCREDIBLE.
AN ANOMALY.

A DECISION. A CHOICE.
THAT'S EXTRAORDINARY.

CHAPTER 39

BIG IDEA!
BUSINESS PARTNER RELATIONSHIPS

"I always believed an extraordinary leader is someone who leads with a spirit of respect, humility, and conviction. It is in this spirit and with these qualities that a vision becomes transformed, setting the tone for success – in life or in business."

– Diana Mann, Associate Publisher, *Consumer Goods Technology* Magazine

---

Business partner relationships are a priority. They must be a priority. Without them it is virtually impossible to move the ball forward on major projects and strategic initiatives requiring skill sets and talent not readily available *within* the organization. The question to consider is this: *How do you value and approach these relationships?*

Each of the roles in my career has involved managing relationships: With retail customers and prospects, consulting partners and agencies, software vendors, strategic integrators, hardware providers, and system support organizations. I find it interesting that some customers or buyers feel it is their privilege or *right* to treat agencies and solution providers like second-class citizens versus true business partners. I just don't get it.

It's not professional or appropriate for an extraordinary organization seeking an extraordinary partnership. This is a basic idea, but the way you treat others will manifest itself well beyond today.

BRINGING IT TO LIFE

◉ **Relationship First, Business Second:** I was recently at lunch with two members of a small consulting organization. Within 15 minutes of sitting down at the table, one of the individuals stated, "We just want you to get us in on the next deal." He knew nothing about me, my team, or my organization. He knew nothing about our strategies or objectives. He knew nothing about my personal goals or interests in moving the organization forward. Clearly, he only cared about *the deal.* Relationships are absolutely the key to success in selling. You can work for the best organization in the country and still lose a deal because you fail to invest in knowing the buyer, their teams and organization, and the culture for successful partnership. Relationship first, business second.

◉ **Relationships Are Not Built Via Email Spam:** When I register for industry events, I fully expect the onslaught of spam from unknown solution providers. They're the ones who have paid for the email address list and are often sponsors of the event. They are looking to make a quick sale. I typically receive an email asking me when I can meet with them for 30 minutes so that they can solve all of my business problems. What a waste. Not extraordinary. These emails go straight to the trash folder. No investment in the relationship yields no meeting.

◉ **Partners – Not Vendors:** Marketing agencies, consulting teams, contract technology staff, HR leadership development consultants, and other service providers are on-site to help the business grow, change, and evolve. They are being paid to accomplish what the organization cannot do with the existing staff and/or internal resources. So why do some customers insist on treating vendors with vitriol, suspicion, dislike, and contempt? I have been on both sides of this coin. It doesn't benefit anyone to treat partners poorly. Keep in mind that the world is small and the golden rule applies inside of work as well as outside of work: Treat others the way you would like to be treated.

◉ **Networks Open Doors – Trusts Wins Partnerships:** Networking is a great way to get into new accounts. Trust between the product, service, solution provider, and the client or customer, is the key to winning partnerships and establishing a long-term recurring revenue stream. You don't just win a deal because you know John who knows Suzy who knows Dan. Relationships absolutely help Dan feel more comfortable about meeting with you, but you must extend trust *to* Dan to win trust *from* Dan. Networks open doors for *meetings* and trust secures *long-term partnership* potential.

- ◉ **Do Your Homework:** "Can you tell us about your strategic priorities for the next twelve months, or any planned projects you have on the docket?" This question is a recipe for a short meeting. There is no purpose in meeting if you are on a fishing expedition. Do your homework. Make assumptions. Determine key investments planned for the organization, hot topics, business priorities, technology plans, etc. One of the traits I value most in great business development executives is when they have done their homework on the organization, related solutions (or industry solutions), and even know something about my background. Bring something to the table besides simply the rod and reel.

- ◉ **Be Willing To Invest:** Consider what you are willing to invest to get your foot in the door. If you have never done work for a specific corporation, it can be difficult to get your foot in the door in a strategic partnership role. Consider offering resources, time, or solutions to *prove* your value to buyers within the organization. Be willing to invest.

◉ **Be Prepared:** I learned this simple concept when I was an Eagle Scout. Not one Scout meeting went by without having to repeat this slogan over and over again. Being prepared means having an agenda, distributing it prior to the meeting, ensuring that attendee lists (names, titles, roles) are communicated ahead of the meeting, action items and key points are documented during the meeting, and notes are distributed after the meeting. Own it.

BOTTOM LINE

When you invest in them, they invest in you.

EXCEPTIONAL. REMARKABLE.
PHENOMENAL. UNUSUAL.
IMPACTFUL. INCOMPARABLE.
WONDERFUL. NOTABLE. MARVELOUS.
LIMITLESS. FANTASTIC. CURIOUS.
OUTSTANDING. DIFFERENTIATED.
OVER-THE-TOP. UNCOMMON.
SINGULAR. SURPRISING. SPECIAL.
ASTONISHING. RARE. UNIQUE.
UNPRECEDENTED. AMAZING. VIVID.
STRONG. MEMORABLE. INCREDIBLE.
AN ANOMALY.

A DECISION. A CHOICE.
THAT'S EXTRAORDINARY.

CHAPTER 40

BIG IDEA!
MOVE FAST

"Extraordinary leadership is rare. Not everyone can focus entirely on their strengths and not their weaknesses."

– Alex Torrez, Vice President, Business Relations, Lawrence Music Group

---

In the last two chapters, we talked about the differentiators in your approach to solving customer business problems as a key factor in delivering extraordinary results. Another key element to differentiating yourself is making things happen *quickly*. You must take advantage of an entry point, a wedge, and any opening. Fast and efficient engagement and follow-up are not core competencies of most large organizations, and that means there is an immediate opportunity for you to act. There is an open door for you to differentiate yourself and to win.

One of the biggest challenges inherent in any large organization is the *lack of* ability to move fast. This is a challenge for a "run-and-gun" team looking to make things happen and drive growth in the business. In customer development, one frequent challenge is that the engagement and follow-up process is never as important to supporting organizations and teams as it is to the actual customer-facing team. They must feel the sense of urgency and recognize the limited window that may exist to achieve results. The organizations that truly win are those that have a nimble, responsive, and engaged supporting cast. This includes legal, finance, supply chain, and the leadership team who may be needed in collaboration with a partnership arrangement.

In developing customer relationships, speed in follow-up is an absolute differentiator versus the competition. It means getting answers to questions today, not tomorrow. It means turning around requests same day. It means negotiating the financial aspects of a contract collaboratively, versus the epic back and forth, used car salesman process. It means returning calls on the same day. It means moving a contract through development and review expediently, and exceeding the expectations of the customer. It means working through internal politics and roadblocks quickly, versus waiting for a standard process or multi-week timeline to play out.

At the end of the day, it is the customer who is the priority; and they don't care about your own internal process issues or inefficiencies. They are interested in solutions that help them to move their business forward. Your internal issues must be transparent to them. Many times the internal processes are not fast enough or efficient enough to support big business ideas. And many times the supporting cast does not understand the pressure inherent in the supplier-prospect relationship. They have never been on the front line, in the board room, or on the phone with an irritated prospect threatening to call the competition.

You can win on speed. Being faster and more responsive than the competition can be a critical differentiator. It proves that you want the business and that you have the internal processes to get things done. It shows that you can clear roadblocks and bring value to the customer, both at the start of the relationship and into the future. It shows you are able to deliver *beyond* the pace that is inherent within most large organizations.

For example, after the pursuit of a major consulting project where we were not selected, I continued to stay in touch with the key-decision maker at the company after he initiated work with the competition. He frequently would reach out to me with questions on business programs and strategies that he was not able to glean from his selected partner. Without hesitation, I would quickly turn around insights and responses. I knew the competition failed in this area, and while a small thing, this simple act of being a great business partner, a responsive and knowledgeable friend, eventually yielded positive results. We were selected for the next piece of business – an even larger opportunity than the first. I invested in him and we developed a level of trust that went beyond a single, simple transaction.

One word of caution: as the leader, if you run fast, it is important to recognize the impact it has on others on the team. Some may think you are doing their job, getting into their business, have little confidence in them, or not allowing them to lead. Recognize the value of teaching, coaching, and mentoring to pick up the total team pace and set a faster cadence in which to operate.

BRINGING IT TO LIFE

◉ **Set The Pace:** As the leader, it is your responsibility to set the pace for the organization. You must coach, nurture, and strongly encourage timelines that may not initially be comfortable to everyone on the team. You will never have 100% of the facts before making decisions. And waiting even for 98% of the facts to come together before sending a follow-up email, making a call, sending a proposal, or making a deal decision just does not work. The competition is slow. You must be fast. You may, at times, make mistakes. Speed keeps the fire hot, continues the momentum, keeps the dialogue moving, and keeps the plane in the air when headwinds are pushing it toward a stall. *What are you doing to set the pace?*

◎ **Recognize The Pace Of Others:** The reality is that a fast pace and a multi-priority work environment is just not in the comfort zone for some individuals. As a leader in a fast-moving, growing organization, it is your responsibility to move these individuals to roles where the pace fits their capacity. As an individual contributor, it is *your* responsibility to recognize where pace does not fit with your capacity and make a change if necessary.

◎ **Fast Follow-Up:** This is a low-hanging fruit opportunity, and we have covered this several times throughout this book. Because so few are good at this, you can really make a powerful, immediate impact by employing *fast follow-up*. Try it. Challenge yourself to turn things around same day. Connect online, offline, and in person, *immediately* following initial introductions. Challenge internal business process timelines. Most people are looking to *get* – figure out what you can *give*.

BOTTOM LINE
Move fast. Don't look back!

EXCEPTIONAL. REMARKABLE.
PHENOMENAL. UNUSUAL.
IMPACTFUL. INCOMPARABLE.
WONDERFUL. NOTABLE. MARVELOUS.
LIMITLESS. FANTASTIC. CURIOUS.
OUTSTANDING. DIFFERENTIATED.
OVER-THE-TOP. UNCOMMON.
SINGULAR. SURPRISING. SPECIAL.
ASTONISHING. RARE. UNIQUE.
UNPRECEDENTED. AMAZING. VIVID.
STRONG. MEMORABLE. INCREDIBLE.
AN ANOMALY.

A DECISION. A CHOICE.
THAT'S EXTRAORDINARY.

CHAPTER 41

BIG IDEA!
FLY NAVY!

"Extraordinary leadership means accomplishing an audacious task . . . when nobody on the team realized you were the one leading them."

– Alvin Townley, Author of *Legacy of Honor* (2007),
Spirit of Adventure (2009), and *Fly Navy* (2011)

One more chapter that centers on extraordinary leadership from a different perspective! As I mentioned earlier, I grew up as the son of a United States Army MEDEVAC helicopter pilot and my mom served in the Navy. So, from a young age, I was fully interested in and passionate about all things flying. After school and during summer breaks, I would regularly work part-time stints in the hanger at Coastal Aviation at Tallahassee's regional airport. I would clean up planes, help the crew maintain aircraft, and manage the hangar. Of course I was always "in" for any planned flights or journeys when an extra seat presented itself. I attended Space Camp annually as a teen and began studying for my private pilot's license. I had developed a passion for flying and enjoyed learning about the space program.

The possibilities "out there" were exciting to consider.

In evaluating college choices, I looked at programs that offered Navy and Air Force ROTC, as they were possible routes to becoming a pilot and working with the space program. I also considered programs that offered co-op or work-study opportunities in order to potentially work within a related area, while still pursuing my degree. Ultimately, I pursued the co-op route and spent three years working on four space shuttles for NASA at the Kennedy Space Center in Florida. This was an amazing experience, especially for someone who chased these dreams as a kid! I was as close to space as I could get without lighting the two solid rocket boosters.

After college I pursued different business routes, yet the passion for all things with wings never left me. In 2011, one of my friends, Alvin Townley, penned a book on the Navy experience entitled *Fly Navy*[4]. It is a great read and brings to life the day-to-day experiences of leading in the Navy. I found a number of striking ideas that applied directly to my findings in the business environment.

The first was the concept of *coasting*. Alvin outlined that, ". . . in the business of flying a *Blue Angel*, coasting or losing the edge can lead to disaster." So is the case in the business world. Extraordinary leaders and their respective teams have little room to coast, little room to lay off a pursuit, and little room not to be extraordinarily detailed and fast in follow-up. We all know *coasters*. We must ensure they are not weighing down the high-octane team.

The second concept centered on the seven skills that prevent mishaps: *decision-making, assertiveness, mission analysis, communication, leadership, adaptability, and situational awareness.* These resounded immediately with me, as there is no doubt that these are core traits to extraordinary leadership. Each of these applies not only to flying Navy jets, but also to leading an organization. Think about it. Leaders need to make decisions quickly and insightfully; need to complete post-mission or post-project analysis; need to communicate frequently; and need to be aware of the situation which surrounds them. These are great concepts to review and a great read in Alvin's book. Another one of my favorite quotes from his book is this: "Your background doesn't matter in the military. With a good set of morals and drive, you can do anything." How true.

Here's how I translated a few of Alvin's *Fly Navy* ideas into *Be Extraordinary!* ideas.

BRINGING IT TO LIFE

◉ **Decision-Making:** This is the ability to assess a situation, understand the trade-offs, and make a timely decision that results in a positive outcome. Many organizations and leaders of organizations get hung up in the politics of not wanting to make a *bad* decision, and therefore make *no* decision. Extraordinary leaders make decisions and learn from the outcomes.

◉ **Assertiveness:** Extraordinary leaders provide a perspective. They share ideas, define solutions to problems, step in when others fail to step up, and are more than willing to lead when others are not. *Do you have the confidence and the assertiveness to step up when no one else is willing?*

◉ **Mission Analysis:** Perhaps one of the greatest opportunities for organizations is to make project or initiative analysis and assessment, part of a management routine. Pause to define what value the work created. Take the time to understand what did not work. Outline steps to make it better and make it best. We talked earlier in the book about lessons learned and after-action reviews. *Is this part of your routine? How often do you complete a major initiative and never look back to review results and outline improvement opportunities?*

◉ **Communication:** In the world of supporting combat operations, there is no room for communication failure. I have found that my own personal failures have occurred when I dropped the ball on communication. Every leader has different expectations regarding communication, and it is important to understand and align these expectations very early in the working relationship. It's a simple conversation and one that is often missed in the early stages of a working relationship. That's because we often assume that others communicate in a way that matches our own style.